The Death of Race

The Death of Race

Building a New Christianity in a Racial World

Brian Bantum

Fortress Press
Minneapolis

THE DEATH OF RACE
Building a New Christianity in a Racial World

Cover design: Brad Norr

Library of Congress Cataloging-in-Publication Data
Print ISBN: 978-1-5064-0888-0
eBook ISBN: 978-1-5064-0889-7

The paper used in this publication meets the minimum requirements of
American National Standard for Information Sciences — Permanence of
Paper for Printed Library Materials, ANSI Z329.48-1984.

Manufactured in the U.S.A.

This book was produced using Pressbooks.com, and PDF rendering was
done by PrinceXML.

To Caleb, Ezra, and Joseph

Because your bodies hold many stories.

Because your bodies are bearers of God.

Contents

Contents

Preface

Every summer, after classes have ended and before I begin any writing projects, I build something. It has become something of a yearly ritual. I put my books away, leave the computer off, and pull my tools from the corner of the garage where they've been sitting for eleven months. It's usually a bookshelf, or a cabinet. At first I was just a poor grad student who needed someplace to put books and papers.

The feeling of wood going smooth, after a few passes with the sander, a pile of wood becoming structure and purpose, the smell of my work sticking to my clothes and hair when I was done for the day—there was something grounded about this work after a year of working with words and ideas. Building was a balm, a sign that I could touch and see, reminding me throughout the year that small steps accumulate, that it is possible to go from ideas into something that was real.

But with every summer I had to start again. I didn't build the same set of bookshelves again and again. It was a twelve-foot-high, floor-to-ceiling bookcase one year, a built-in media cabinet another. Each summer was a new space in the house, a new set of problems and skills unique to that project.

I am a novice builder, so I did the best I could and learned from my mistakes.

Having built something myself, my eye was drawn again and again to true craftsmanship. A set of library shelves, or a table with beveled edges, or a chair that fit your back just right. Great carpenters build for the space, for what is needed in *that* house in *that* corner. They don't make the same shelf for every job.

The last four summers have begun with the familiar drone of sanders and saws. But these projects were also followed, almost liturgically, with outrage and lament as our family watched the succession of black men and women killed by police. We'd follow the news and seemingly inevitable nonindictments. July and August would be cycles of well-worn tropes of "black on black crime" and white guilt then backlash, and another murder and another exoneration. And then fall came with a new academic year.

I would return to teaching, and to welcome students to the task and beauty of theology. Early in my teaching it took time for students to see the significance of race, of gender, of the ways bodies had been so violently divided. But now they returned not needing to be convinced. And they wanted theology to matter. The theologies that had been built for them did not fit the space they now lived in. They had questions. What they witnessed over those summers, what they had seen (or not seen) in their congregations seemed inadequate. For others, especially my students of color, they returned to campus with grief and anger that their theologies could not name.

They did not lack desire or commitment. What I found in my conversations with them was that, at its heart, their Christianity rarely accounted for their bodies, their difference. Race, gender, sexuality, differing abilities. These everyday realities of their lives rarely intersected with conversations about Jesus and salvation, or even what it means to be human.

Initially, I did not want to write this book, yet another book on race. There are pastors, activists, and scholars whose voices are speaking to policies, theories, theologies, and histories in powerful ways. But the more time I have spent with my students, the more I have come to believe that we need to build something new, something that speaks to our moment, that can faithfully narrate Christianity in a racial world, but also account for gender, for the differences inherent in our bodies. This book is not about *how* to build a "new" Christianity. This book is an offering, a prayer. It is the sketch of a new shelf that might fit our space, our moment. I am not building from nothing. I am breaking boards and prying out old nails, cutting and sanding from the shelves and chairs and tables of saints that have walked before. But I am building for now, for my children, my students, for myself. It is a theology written as if our bodies mattered—mattered in our very creation, in our fall, in our redemption, and in our following. It is a starting point for people who want to tell a new story about their God, their bodies and lives together.

Acknowledgments

This book is clearer and richer because of Amey Victoria Adkins and Sarah Keough, who offered insightful critique and questions. This book would not have been possible without the support of Seattle Pacific University, which granted me a sabbatical to write and sit with this text. My friend and colleague, Jeff Keuss, exemplifies what it means to create space for others and imagine an ever-widening community of faithful witnesses. My editor, Lisa Gruenisen, continued to press for the book she knew I could write when I wanted to settle. Above all, this book bears the indelible wisdom of my wife, Pastor Gail Song Bantum, whose question continued to guide and afflict me as I wrote. "Who is this book for?" she said. Prayerfully, I am writing for my people, and whoever feels the call to walk with us on the way.

1

Race Is a Story Written on My Body

"You have to choose. Pick a box, white or black," my mother told me in the lobby of the bank, the blank social security form laid out on the glass table. "It doesn't really mean anything. It's just a government form, but you can only choose one," she said. But, for a six-year-old everything has meaning. So I considered my mom and dad. I considered myself, lighter skin than my brother and father, straight auburn hair like my mother. To be real, I liked her better. "White," I said after these quick calculations. But of course it didn't have any meaning. "Black," my brother chose after doing his own internal math. This was the first moment I began to *tell* the story of my body, when I began to feel that my body was a story.

My mother wanted to believe that my decision didn't have any meaning. But of course it did. The story took shape in small ways at first, ways that I didn't intend. Somehow I found myself in its pages. I would read its words. The words of race would read me.

"Why you talk like that?" We were all hanging on monkey bars during recess.

Me? "Talk like what? I talk like my mom and dad. Why do *you* talk like that?" I saw a "me" instead of an "us."

There were innocent middle school crushes and a few notes from girls whose skin was like mine, brown eyes, brown hair. They saw me as I walked through the halls, looked at me in ways the little white girls didn't. Were they like me? Was I like them? I'm ashamed to admit it, but I didn't think so at the time. Like most kids that try to navigate the purgatory of middle school, I tried to say who I was by being sure of what I wasn't. This is how we all come to understand who we are—drawing lines of similarity and distinction, conjuring an image of ourselves and doing our best to live into that image or resist it.

High school cafeterias held the usual questions. Where to sit? Who were my people? Race was an abyss. And something had changed in me. My hair did not hang down my face or part on the left. It had begun to curl and stand atop my head. It was unwieldy, alien, the first sign that I was not what I thought I was. In the midst of disorientation I found my way with a hasty kind of echolocation, throwing out sounds and listening for what bounced back—feeling and looking for difference, for safe places to continue swimming forward. I discovered that darker kids saw my body like theirs, even if I didn't yet. "You're black. Work on the MLK assembly with us."

Me? "I guess." I still feel the tremble when the first chord of "Lift Every Voice" sounded in my chest. This came from *my* people? I didn't walk toward the sound right away. It would take a Korean American woman to help me discover what it meant to be black.

We were nineteen and had a mutual friend who thought we'd connect. I called Gail Song on the phone and, I'll be honest, I thought I was talking to a black girl. (She probably thought she was talking to a white guy.) There was something in her cadence. She echoed the tremble I had heard in the hymn on MLK Day. She was a child of the in-between, too.

Gail was the child of Korean immigrants and grew up poor in a northern suburb of Chicago. Her friends were the "dark" kids who clung together in a sea of whiteness. On Sunday and Wednesday nights her family drove into the city to their Korean Pentecostal church for all-night prayer or Bible study. "You full Korean?" the grandmothers would ask her because her skin was a little darker and her eyes just a little deeper set. The echo in her voice came from the black church, though. When she could choose for herself she sought out her people, and she found them in the black Pentecostal churches.

We met in person for the first time two months after that first call and many letters later. Gail was beautiful. Deep tanned skin, brown eyes and hair with streaks of blond, big hoop earrings, and a laugh that poured joy into the room. She was driven and fun, gospel and classical. She was truly Pentecostal, speaking in many tongues.

To know her was to be drawn into two worlds. The first was the life of the black church. I just tried not to stare the first few times. This was not my Southern Baptist Church in Maryland. Gail swayed, clapped on the backbeat, knew when to "Amen" and when to "Yaasss." I remember thinking then that this woman was blacker than I would ever be.

But she also drew me into the world of Korean Americans, kimchee and bulgogi, cold-spicy noodles and never wearing shoes in the house; hanging back at the after-church potluck until most people have filled their plates and getting to the waiter first to pay the check at dinner. I was immersed in the tensions of becoming American, wanting to be seen as American, and I came to see that racism wasn't just a white thing. I saw that we were all caught in the story.

I'm sure she'd say I drew her into a new world too, butter and salad dressing, sharing your feelings and TV. I'm still not sure it was a fair exchange. In meeting Gail I discovered a freedom to explore the story of that tremble I had felt in high school, that I saw in her and felt in church. W. E. B. Du Bois, Frederick Douglass, Henry Highland Garnett, Ida B. Wells, David Walker, Sojourner Truth; I discovered the terror and the power of the black story, of my story, and how my mixed body was threaded into this long history.

Race is this act of conjuring. As our lives entwined I began to feel the currents of race flow around us. I was undergoing a conversion, of sorts. I could not name it at the time, but when I was nineteen and began to read the history of my body and this word, race—and its children: white, black—I began to see the way I had been its unwitting disciple. I followed its precepts and sought its appeasement. My desires, my loves were shaped by it. To become black would require a conversion.

I began to see new stories, new modes of being, new joys and imperfections. I saw myself inside this racial story, as a carrier of its truth and pain. To be black was to walk inside a struggle, a pressure that sought to name, encountered by declarations of what I was not or could not be. But to be black was also to survive, resist, overcome. Joy and flourishing could be revolutionary.

Race is not a history. Race is the story of our bodies, of our churches, of our faith. Race is a story that shapes the idea of what our bodies are for. It is a word that has de-created our world and us. Enacting an amazing capacity to name and to classify, to build and to use, our bodies have been drawn into a colonial idolatry where relationships, communities, nations are shaped by an idolatrous idea made flesh in our everyday lives. It might have begun with colonial ships, but it persists and marks us all. Whether we are old to America or new to this land, race encompasses all of our lives and we must navigate its effects on a daily basis. We are telling the story or we are resisting the story, but we cannot leave its pages.

We are all participating in the story of race. It is ubiquitous. It has shaped how we live, who we live with, how we see others, and how we see ourselves. Some suggest we should just become post-racial, as though we can train ourselves to see something other than race. But there will always be something, some difference that we use to justify the privilege of some and the suffering of others.

When I married Gail I saw how this story was not just a story of white and black. Her mother arrived in America at twenty-two and had to navigate language and neighborhood and food. Bananas and Chef Boyardee was what it meant to be American. Her father did not venture as far out into this new land, staying close to Korean neighborhoods and within Korean churches. But for Gail there was another level of complexity. The language of her home was not the language of her friends. The food of her home was not the food of her friends. At school she was asked, "Where are you from? No, where are you really from?"—every day the perpetual foreigner. She had to navigate how people interpreted her face as foreign even if America is the only place she had ever known.

But even as I heard the stories of alienation among Korean Americans I also sensed the divide between Korean Americans and black communities. Despite our mutual alienation, the story of race still wrote our bodies apart.

After we were married, Gail and I faced a decision every time we moved to a new city. Where should we go to church? The black nondenominational church, the multicultural charismatic church? the Korean American church? The question of race and faith were always intertwined.

When I was sixteen I became a Christian. When I was nineteen I became black. Christian identity and racial identity were never far apart in my life. They were both words and ideas that walked and talked and touched, meanings and truths bound to my body. I first encountered the enfleshing, the embodiment of Christian identity in the transformation of my father. Growing up he was a kind man, but yoked to the bottle. He wasn't violent, but he was barely present. By the time I was eight he and my mom had divorced, even as they remained friends. I saw him choose little things over my brother and me, my mother. I saw him as the cause of my mother's loneliness and pain. But when I was fifteen I came home and was surprised to see him sitting at the kitchen table with Mom. He had cancer. Stage four. Three months to live.

He came to live with us and I discovered he had gotten sober. He was a Christian now. But I could feel his peace, even in my confusion. I found myself encountered by a God who speaks, becomes present through broken, imperfect people.

Jesus did not meet me in a dream or in a book or in a thought dropped from space. God encountered me in hugs and embraces and grief and mourning and laughter. God met me in potlucks and people who called me by my name. And in these people I met a God who became like me, who desired me so deeply that the difference between finitude and infinity was not so wide that this God could not traverse it to be with me, to be like me so that I could be a bit more like God, to be with God. In those teenage years I came to understand myself as Christian and black, two claims that I am still living into, still trying to discern what faithfulness looks like.

But in this journey I have come to understand that race and faith are not distinct, separate questions. That I thought they could be is the byproduct of a certain Christian story, a Christian story that bears responsibility for the racism and sexism and violence of our world. It may not be the root cause, but there were not just guns and slaves on the boats that carried colonizers to the New World. There were Bibles, too.

Our world is indelibly marked by race, by violent differentiations of ethnicity, culture, and gender. I have no use for a Christianity that does not account for the ways our bodies are named and shaped. The ways we name our bodies and actions are never innocent and innocuous; our words matter. Our bodies do work. Every day I am encountered by a world that tries to name me. My very existence, my breathing and laughing and writing, arises out of a Word, a Word that authors all that I am. The relationship between words and bodies is not a voluntary area of consideration. For a Christian, it is *the* question of our identity.

If Christianity can separate the bodily questions that shape or misshape our everyday lives it is not a faith of the incarnate Word; it is a lie, a lie that denies our stories, our bodies, and how our bodies do work in the world.

We are stories. To say we are a story is not to suggest we create ourselves. Poetry, fiction, art is not about telling falsehoods, but speaking the truth. But we do not need fiction to tell stories about who we are and why we are. To say that identity, faith, or race is a story is to say that we are a product of history and that we participate in that history. We cannot extricate ourselves from it, but neither are we slaves to it. When I chose "white" on that form at six years old I began to tell a story about who I was. I retold that story as I tried to explain to others (to myself) why I didn't talk like the other black kids or listen to the same music as my brother. But eventually I would have to see myself truthfully. I would have to tell another story about my body. I would have to tell my story alongside the body of my wife and eventually my children. But like my baptism, the Christian symbol of participating in Jesus's death and resurrection, I must name the story that is being put to death. I must struggle to discern what must die and what must live even as I emerge from the water, a new person. This is the call to discipleship. But this is not just a story of my spiritual identity. There are other stories that have shaped my body and my life: the story of race, the story of gender, the story of nation and class. These stories are woven into us, thread-by-thread, commercial-by-commercial, neighborhood-by-neighborhood, and sermon-by-sermon. What is the story of race that has shaped us? How can the Christian story help us to see ourselves, and one another, in more faithful ways? And even more, how can we live for one another's fullness and flourishing?

Our identities are about our bodies. Who we are is bound to how we live. I cannot call myself a soccer player and walk onto a basketball court with ice skates and a volleyball and hope to have anyone recognize me as a soccer player. To be a soccer player I choose certain clothes. Through hours of training I even develop a certain walk; I tend toward certain foods and away from others. I use shorthand words and I tend to see certain people because of my training schedule and I tend to not see others. A culture emerges around these patterns, and when my children are born they eat, sleep, and breathe these patterns until they are not a choice, but simply a way of being. To be a soccer player is to be human, to be human is to walk this way, talk this way, eat this way. After a while I don't need the names to do the work. The walk does work. The talk does work. Who I am announces itself as I enter the room without saying a word. My body does work. These dynamics are not just individual but social and systemic. The way we read one another's bodies is connected to the ways our society has valued some bodies and devalued others. Media, neighborhoods, education all participate in this process of drawing us into a racial world.

Christianity is about a body that does work. It is a confession that arises from a people who speak of the creation of humanity as bearing God's very image, that our bodies are wonderful and beautiful. It is a confession that we were made for community and relationship and that our bodies are what make this image possible. It is a confession that arises from a God who is utterly different than creation. The ease with which we worship in racially and ethnically distinct churches in this country belies a tragic truth. In America, Jesus is only occasionally the center of Christian identity, especially for those who seem to utter his name so often. Too often, Christian identity in America is more about bodies governed by a racial ideal in the guise of a so-called Christianity. Race is more determinative for our lives than being a Christian. Race shapes who marries who, where we live and cannot live, who is more likely to be seen as guilty or innocent, who shapes our prospects for education or health. Race permeates our existence in this country. This story is not simply about a few bad apples or an abstract notion of sin. This is about a Christian story that has not accounted for the body of Jesus or the bodies of those who believe.

More than twenty years from those two life-transforming conversions, racial and Christian identities are inseparable in my world. Both of these conversions required death so that I might find life. Envy. Lust. Jealousy. Insecurity. Greed. Cowardice. Embracing the life of Christ meant being willing to identify the aspects of my life that were so contrary to the peace of God's life, so contrary to the image of God knit into me from the beginning of time and reconstituted in me through Christ's birth, life, death, and resurrection.

But maybe these were the easy things to see. When encountered by the history of my blackness something else had to die—the lie of my independence, of my autonomy, of my life only being my own. I was part of a people. My story was bound up on multiple sides of this tragic encounter, but I could not extricate myself from it. I would have to open my eyes to the ways I had been formed by the story, by the ways that I resisted and participated.

In awakening to my blackness I was also reborn in my faith. The living God, the God of flesh and blood, encountered me in new ways. There was more I needed to repent for than lies and lust. There was something else in me that needed to die. I had to awaken to the ways racial supremacy had shaped me, how it had formed me to see poverty or crime as individual issues rather than systemic problems. I had to awaken to how media and schools and friendships had shaped me. I had to awaken to the ways my manhood authorized my voice while others were silenced or ignored. I had to awaken to see again an incarnate God who was not like me, a poor Jewish child conceived to an unwed mother in a colonized land.

But perhaps most of all, I was reborn into a realization that my body does work in this world. When I teach, when I walk down the street, my body is speaking and these words are powerful. But just like a disciple, I cannot know the meaning of these words fully. I must learn to listen and follow and deepen my understanding of the language that I am being taught to speak and live.

God wants us to be free. The heart of Christian confession is that God abhors the deaths we are subjected to. Scripture is the testament to God's continual desire for us to be alive, to love and be loved, to be with God and with one another. In our deluded sense of independence God reminds us of our essential relationality. In our exile or imprisonment God comes near. In the midst of our violation of others' bodies, bodies made in the image of God, God becomes like us, makes bodied life a part of God's own life. For lives repeatedly alienated through a thousand little comments or rendered invisible by society, God sees and names and touches. In the midst of these the incarnation is God's Word to us that our bodies were made to be free and to love.

When I read Scripture, encounter activists, hear poets, I am reminded that God desires our bodies to be free. God becomes like us so that we can become like God—so that we might love one another, be with one another, that our lives might mirror and participate in the community that is God's life. This freedom is a bodily freedom. It is a freedom that animates where I live, who I marry, what vocations I aspire to. Freedom is the possibility of living a life without being perceived as a threat wherever I go, or having to prove that I might have something to contribute. Freedom is the possibility of discovering who I was created to be, which is enough of a challenge without the explicit and implicit messages that my body is an exception to what is beautiful, good, and wise.

Our world thwarts God's goodness, subjects one another's bodies to terror and abuse. Race, in particular, permeates so many of our contemporary terrors. The confluence of colonialism and whiteness (its supremacy and sovereignty) completely reshaped the world. The American slave system and current criminal justice system, global media, explosions of cosmetic surgeries that exalt Western myths of beauty, the persistence of whitening creams, postcolonial violence, and the seemingly unending cycle of terrorism and antiterrorism, all churn from the peculiar modern engine that is race.

Race cycles within sexism and patriarchy, arguably the most ancient of systemic sins. Black men who could brilliantly articulate the basis of their freedom would silence black women in their midst who co-built the churches, the marches and movements. White feminists could highlight the patriarchal exclusion of women from educational opportunities or workplace leadership and yet resist critiques that highlighted their complicity in racist structures. The masters' wives were no abolitionists.

To hope for the death of race is not to hope for a post-racial utopia. No, race is not the particular hue of my body or the language I speak. Race is a system, an intuition, a systemic reflex that seeks to decipher who can use who. It is an imaginative frame that justifies the death of the Native and the violence of the colonist, the deportation of the Mexican worker and the citizenship of the Irish refugee. Race is a way of resisting difference by violently determining which differences matter. Race is about power, sovereignty, and how words can become enfleshed, part of our daily, bodily lives, shaping who we are.

We resist the words that are being spoken over us, seek different ways of stating who we are or should be. But even our refusals participate in this world because they have to respond to what has been said. Race is an illusion, a falsehood, a creation of man. Yes, but it is a creation the way "America" is a creation, a falsehood. Once there was a time when this land was called by other names, with different expectations of faithfulness. But now it is called America and some of its people "Americans" and others "alien." These names are now part of our story. Race lives now and we cannot simply return to a time before America, before whiteness or blackness. We cannot go back to the Native peoples and ask them what we should call it or how we should live. There are too many dead, too many roads, too many homes, and too many new names.

We will always be children of this racial world, even if race is long dead. But perhaps resurrection is possible. It created the world we live in. As disciples we follow, we live into a vision of truth. We develop practices and ways of seeing the world. We do not always live into these words faithfully, but they shape how we think we should live, what we should hope for, and what we think we do or don't deserve.

Christian discipleship is life found in death. Perhaps Christian discipleship offers us a way forward because its life is found in death, even if what must die is not always for us to determine. Discipleship is a rediscovery of our bodies and lives; a life of following is entering into the mystery of what it means that God has made us in the image of

13

God. Discipleship is a wrestling with the ways that our lives have been so deeply determined and deformed by this racial word that we can only begin by naming the death that it has brought to all of us. Like unknowing believers on the precipice of a baptismal pool, we must submit our bodies to death, even if we do not know what will still be alive when we emerge from the water.

In the beginning of our world there was a word. Its syllables were European ships crossing the sea, leathers ripped from dark bodies and replaced with button suits, chains clinging in cargo holds, and the moans and cries of dark bodies whose life was again and again twisted out. The world we live in now is intertwined with words uttered by men with the power to create a distorted order. Their words did not create like God creates, however. Theirs were words of de-creation, creating themselves by the death of the world that encountered them. It was an exercise of fear and hubris. We exist in the shadow of a moment where this hubris was not familial or local. The colonists shaped the entire globe. Wherever the ships went, they took with them a view of themselves that had no room for difference. In this way, race is an incarnation, of sorts. Race is the embodiment of an idea that was brought into world. Race is the water out of which we are all born.

The death of race. But in the face of this terrifying truth it is also important to say that my body is not a race. Race is the structure of death, the dehumanizing and de-creating word a people sought to speak over the world, and violently succeeded. Race is what overshadows the world, conceiving our bodies and their differences as something to be perpetually overcome. Race is like cancer, a cell that shares a likeness to part of my world, and yet because of the slightest variance in its structure, it multiplies violently in my body until I am overrun and overdetermined by how it sees me, a body to be consumed.

I will not survive these deformed cells, this de-creating word, race, by pretending it does not exist. We cannot pretend that it is not there lying dormant in every body. No, I can only survive and prayerfully flourish if I can begin to see what my body is for and what it ought to be, if I can seek the life, relationships, and political organizations that can make that life possible for me and for others. I must first begin with what my body is. Surely I am more than a mind or a soul. Surely being made in the image of God is more than a capacity to name, to determine, to cut, hew, and build.

And I will not survive the death of race by hoping to simply get past it, to be post-racial. We cannot be post-racial because we cannot be post-story. We cannot escape the story that has formed us or the stories that shape the world we live in. We cannot be post-racial because race is not about the differences that we see. It is about how those differences have come to form who we think we can be for one another. Race is a story bound to the death of certain bodies that continues to exert itself on how we live and hope in this world. Race was a de-creating word, a word that dehumanized and rendered dark bodies into things to be used. We must account for the deaths race has woven into our story as a people. In accounting for its destructive de-creation of the world, we can begin to see how our particular bodies and lives can begin to speak the deepest truth of Christian confession—that God desires us to be free, for one another and for God.

Race is not simply biology or the various physical marks that supposedly distinguish human beings from one another.

Race is a network of ideas and beliefs that become enfleshed in our economy, our social life, and our national imagination. This web traps us in our skins, shapes how we see one another and our world. Death is always a part of race.

"Building" a new Christianity. To face the death of race as Christians we hope to witness to the justice, peace, and love of what God has done in the world through Christ. But like those first creatures who bore God's image in the garden, God calls us to participate, to work, to steward, maybe even to help build. Building could be seen as utilitarian, practical. But what you will find in these pages is not a step-by-step guide to overcoming race and racism. By build I mean to say that what is made requires our participation, our intention, counting the cost. But building is also a process that requires understanding the materials with which we create, the challenges of building in a certain nook or on certain slopes. When I was in grad school I began to build my own bookshelves. I measured the wall's height and length. To be efficient I made a jig and pre-cut the sides and shelves. But when I began to put the shelves together along the wall the pieces did not fit quite right. The wall was actually different heights on each side. As I did more research and worked with other carpenters I discovered that building is about planning and adapting, that you have to measure and cut along the way. It means building as you go, not measuring everything before you begin, but cutting to fit the spaces you have.

Building a new Christianity is not to say we are building from nothing. Building suggests that we find ourselves in the midst of fragmented homes and fallen structures. Some are older and some are more recent, but what we have is somehow not suited to the conditions we find ourselves in, or that we have created for ourselves. So we must build, build from the pieces that have been left to us, both broken and beautiful, scattered pieces and whole foundations, to create a space that can witness to what God has done and is doing in our midst.

I realize that the idea of a new Christianity might seem like a bit of hubris. There is nothing truly new. So when I think of a "new" Christianity I mean a *Christian* sense of new, a baptismal sense of becoming new creatures, where we rise from the waters as newborns. We are not learning the world for the first time. We discover what our lives must look like as we live from the particularity of our bodies and our stories. We must learn the patterns of faithfulness that we are called into and the patterns of unfaithfulness that have formed us or that we continue to live out of. We must discover what to confess about who we are and who God is.

Too many American churches especially have failed to see that far from being an answer, the church has been part of the problem, continuing to construct without recognizing the centrality of the body, the very timbers with which we build. Instead, I hope this is a beginning, a way to reimagine what it is that Christ calls us to in the midst of a world so violently marked by race. In this book I do not offer steps to reconciliation or a radical new world. What I hope for is a way of measuring our space more faithfully, of seeing our bodies and lives more faithfully so that we might know better what must be cut and what can be built together. I hope this book is a way of helping us to see our unfaithfulness, but also begin to see the beauty and gift of what it means to be made in the image of God. I hope that in this book we can begin to see why our bodies, in all of their beautiful particularity, are so important for being made in the image of God, and how race distorts the very quality that allows us to love and live with God, and one another.

2

Bodies Matter

My brother and I always saw difference. We saw the differences of our skin, our hair. We saw who looked more like Mom and who looked more like Dad. These differences didn't mean much in the beginning. But it didn't take long before my brother and I tried to make sense of the differences we saw in each other and the differences we saw in our schools and neighborhoods. By the time I was nine and he was seven a story began to emerge that helped us to explain the differences of our skin and hair. I must have more of Mom in me, I thought. And Kyle must have more of Dad in him, we agreed.

Of course these weren't the only differences we saw in the world. We knew pink dolls weren't for us and that girls weren't as strong as boys, but they were good at other things, like talking, so it all evened out. We tried to make sense of the world, of ourselves. We didn't see souls or inner thoughts. We saw each other's bodies. I looked in the mirror and saw my straightish brown hair, coffee-and-cream skin, and my nose sprinkled with freckles. I saw my brother's almost-chocolate skin and crown of soft black curls, and how girls loved to run their hands through it. I saw how kids who looked like my dad seemed to get in trouble all the time, and I wondered why they didn't talk like him. And people saw my body. I'd get chased around the playground being called "fish-lips," only years later realizing the racist connotation. I knew my body confused people. "What are you?" they would ask.

I asked why. This is part of what makes us such beautiful creatures. We see. We touch. We taste. And we ask questions about what we see and touch and taste. We ask questions about what we experience in the world. "Why?" "How did this come to be?"

When I eventually became a Christian I became part of a church that told a particular creation story, a story about what differences mattered and what God intended for those differences. The story of creation went something like this: God created men and women. Women and men were made for different roles. That's why their bodies are different. Men lead, are independent, heads of the house. Women are emotional, caregivers. We were made with rational minds, capable of making choices. I saw the implications of this story in men's ministries, especially. Missing fathers and their leadership, their strength, was the real reason that so many men, especially dark men, were in jails. The gender and the race questions were connected, it seemed. I'm a little embarrassed to admit this, but it's the story I was told and the story I believed when I was a young Christian, just beginning my walk. None of us are free from the stories that form us.

But eventually this story could not explain the world I was living in. I went to college and became a history major. The story my church told me could not explain Gail, the powerful, wise woman I would meet my sophomore year at Messiah College. It couldn't explain my mother or my aunts, all strong intelligent women. It couldn't account for the many other ways our bodies were seen and counted and discounted.

That creation story was a way of naming what was *natural* to us, what we should be and what we should be seeking. It was a way of naming our bodies, our humanity, what we were for, and what we were not for.

Beliefs about who we are explicitly or implicitly guide how we navigate and shape our world. We see evidence of these assumptions in documents such as the Declaration of Independence. "Inalienable rights" is a claim about what is natural to us. But it is also a claim about what is natural to others. These indispensable or so-called natural rights did not extend to women, indigenous peoples, African slaves. What was supposedly natural to the dark body? Subservience. Sexual wantonness. Intellectual incapacity.

These stories bore fruit as justification of violence against women or the enslavement of Africans or the genocide against indigenous tribes. We live with the implications of these beliefs in our contemporary moment as well. We see them flare up when two children in a class, one white and one black, speak out of turn. The black child is given detention and the white child's disruption is overlooked or addressed through informal interventions. This moment reveals the implicit way the teacher has been formed to believe that a negative action is expected, almost natural, to the black child, who must therefore be disciplined quickly to "get the child on the right track."[1] Conversely, the white child's action is

---

1. "In 132 Southern school districts, Blacks were disproportionately suspended and expelled at rates five times or higher than their representation in the student population." E. J. Smith and S. R. Harper *Disproportionate impact of K-12 school*

seen as an exception to the rule, something outside of his or her normal behavior and therefore can be overlooked because it will more than likely not happen again. When a police officer pulls over a black man and immediately pulls his gun, there is something happening in the officer's assumption of what that man will do or could do.[2]

The story I learned in that little Baptist church tried to explain how things should be. It gave us a vision for what was wrong in our neighborhoods and our homes. But like my and my brother's explanation for the differences we saw in each other, this creation story of gender roles and colorblindness could not explain the people I saw every day. It could not explain the legacies of enslavement and patriarchy. That first story I learned sheared the realities of our bodies from our souls. Like a sieve, the creation story strained out the pulp and seeds and flesh of our lives until all that was left was a clear, colorless, intangible juice, free of seeds that could create new life, flesh that nourishes and frees me from hunger. It was a story without flesh.

The image of God is a body and difference. Genesis, especially the creation story, has always been one of my favorite books of the Bible to read. When I was sixteen and a new Christian I walked myself two miles to Walden Books to get my first Bible, a New King James Version, just like my dad's, and I started from the beginning. I returned again and again and again. But each time I came back I brought new stories with me. First, were the struggles of Gail as a woman who felt called to ministry and the men who so easily told her that her body rendered her wisdom meaningless. I saw the

suspension and expulsion on Black students in southern states (Philadelphia: University of Pennsylvania, Center for the Study of Race and Equity in Education, 2015).

2. See Naomi Zack, *White Privilege and Black Rights: The Injustice of U.S. Police Racial Profiling and Homicide* (Lanham, MD: Rowman & Littlefield, 2015).

scandal of Rahab and her participating in God's redeeming work. I brought with me images of African slaves chained, black men and women lynched, Japanese families interned, women abused and raped, or simply ignored. I saw Exodus and slave spirituals, women and men who saw their own humanity when their country did not. I saw faith, courage, true humanity.

I returned to Genesis with fleshly stories, people's bodies, their difference seemingly justifying their deaths and dehumanization, even while their survival and their courage displayed our truest humanity. I returned with the same question my brother and I had asked when we were so young, "Why?" "What are we for?"

When I read the story of humanity's beginnings with the weight of these lives pressed into my body, I did not see a story of marriage. I did not see a story that simply explained why I should not have sex before marriage or why women were somehow to blame for the evil in our world. In the moment of humanity's birth I saw a story of God's body, a body of difference, a body where we are not made to be alone, to be singular. We are made to love. We are made plural. I saw the beauty and power of people created different from one another and this difference was a likeness to God, to God's life. In the creation of humanity we see what is most fundamental to being created like God, that we are different from one another and that we are made to be with another. Our bodies are what make this difference and our love for one another possible, incarnate.

The body is love. The creation story is a sign that we were created to be with God and with others. These two creatures that are formed from primordial chaos, formed and breathed into being, beautiful signs of how difference and likeness

23

are tangled together, that we are ground and God, flesh and Spirit, male and female—and that these differences are what make it possible for us to be like God. But perhaps most of all, this creation story is a story that reveals what it means to be free, to be a unique creature in this world, and that being free is not a kind of sovereignty, but rather a profound exercise of love.

Retracing our beginnings is a kind of resistance. It's a way of renaming what is beautiful about our bodies and our lives so that we can see more truthfully what dehumanizes us, and what God hopes for us. If race is a story that becomes manifest in our bodies and lives, different stories must be told and embodied to resist the deathly consequences of this racial story. We must see a new story, a story that gets told in our Sunday schools and youth groups, our Sunday-morning pulpits and small-group meetings. The story of our beginnings is also a story of what should be natural to us, what we are for. The creation story is not simply a story of marriage or obedience and disobedience.

We have to begin here because race seems to permeate so much of our society that the easy answer is to say, "We are all the same underneath." But we are not the same. There is no underneath. While *homo sapiens* refers to shared biological traits, my experiences, my intellect, my emotional life, my relationships, my geographical or national context all shape my understanding of myself and my world in different ways. There is no underlying biological marker that determines who I am going to be apart from the world that has formed me. Who I am is intimately tied to the way my body is seen by others. My identity is shaped by a society that values certain names and sees others as threats.[3] The fact that I have to navigate the world with these ideas makes me unique.

Difference is not something to be feared or explained away. The differences of our bodies and lives are a reality our creation story must make sense of. In this story we begin to see just how vital our body is to a life of love.

As offspring of a mixed-race father, my children cannot experience my life. They will never know life as the son of a white mother and a black father. I cannot reproduce my identity in them. We share a certain sense of being in between, a feeling Gail and I share. These experiences found a home with one another, but this does not mean we are *really* the same underneath. My children, my wife, experience the world in their own ways, and I need those differences to discover who I am and who God is. Every thread of the tapestry of our family might share a braided design, but they have been dyed in different waters that create colors and textures that are unique to them. To honor God's work in them I must acknowledge where the patterns seem consonant, even while recognizing how particularities shift and transform the shape of their lives.

Of course we share fundamental emotions—loss, joy, love. But these hopes and loves and laments are tied to how we each experience the world. When I got married I knew I wasn't binding myself to someone who was just like me underneath. Our marriage was a journey to join our differences together to make something new, discovering how our differences animate and challenge one another in ever-changing ways as we grow in our experience of the world. We are different people. We are not the same

3. Colin Holbrook, Daniel M. T. Fessler, and Carlos David Navarrete, "Looming Large in Others' Eyes: Racial Stereotypes Illuminate Dual Adaptations for Representing Threat Versus Prestige as Physical Size," *Evolution and Human Behavior*. Accessed October 30, 2015.

underneath. Seeing our difference as a theological gift is the beginning of embodying a new story.

The story of race is the story of our bodies, of our bodies' differences. It is a story wrapped up in the differences of gender, race, nation, class, and varying abilities. Creation is a story of difference, of night and day, land and water, animals that fly or swim or walk, human beings and animals, God and humanity, male and female. And all of it is *good*.

What are our bodies for? Before we can begin to think about race and the bodies race creates, we need to ask why our bodies matter, what are they for? God makes us like God and somehow our bodies are important in this likeness. When I was a young Christian I read this story as a marriage story, the first marriage. But not all people are married. We can't even say that marriage is most fundamental to who God is. God creates us to share something with us, and in order to receive this life and love we share a likeness with God. So before there is marriage there is likeness. God says, "Let us make humankind in our image" (Genesis 1:26). And there is difference: "male and female, let us make them" (Genesis 1:27b).

Maybe we could push the story to try to correlate each person to a person in God's life. But this story is not about marriage as what likeness to God means, or even maleness and femaleness somehow associated with the different persons of the Trinity. No, maleness and femaleness are signs, tangible signs of what it means to be like God, to share life with someone who is not like me. Our lives are bound to people whose differences are seen, felt, heard, lived with. But like God, these differences are not competitive or hierarchical, where the weakness of one is necessary to establish the power of the other.

In Adam and Eve the first thing we see are bodies whose likeness to God is revealed as relationship. They are bound to one another, bound to the ground, and bound to God. Who I am cannot be understood without my mother, my brother, my father, my wife, my children, my friends. Even now, with my parents both gone, they constitute something of who I am. Adam is not like God without Eve, and Eve is not like God without Adam. This is not a statement about marriage, but rather about what it means to be human. We are not singular, sovereign, independent individuals. We cannot be like God by ourselves. And this difference is a gift that allows them to love and live within God's life.

Our difference is a gift because it reminds us that we have need, that we are not independent. Imagine Adam waking up and seeing a small cherry tree. He takes a few hesitant bites, tastes its sweetness, and looks forward to the next day when he will eat nothing but cherries from that tree all day. As he looks through the trees he sees a river moving through the forest and finds the perfect spot to sit while he eats. But before he knows it a deep sleep falls upon him. He's asleep for hours and hours and hours. He wakes to find something, someone with him. As this person wakes up Adam finds joy. Two arms, two legs, eyes and a mouth like his. Some slight differences, but they seem to be able to communicate. She looks at him with a certain knowing and he sees himself in her.

So they get up and he takes her to the cherry tree. But along the way they pass an orange tree. She doesn't want to go any further. She bites into the orange and it is the most amazing thing in the world. She doesn't want to eat anything else. But Adam has tasted nothing but those cherries since he woke up. So he says, "Fine. Can we at least take some oranges with us and then get some cherries on the way to the river?" But at the river she says, "There are too many bugs and the water is so loud. Why don't we go to the top of that hill over there? We will be able to see everything that is around us, get to know this new place while we enjoy our oranges." But to Adam it is so far and long and he is already hungry. He says to her, "I thought that when I woke up next to someone who was like me I would have someone to go to the river and eat cherries every day. Why don't you want to eat cherries by the river?" But Eve doesn't want cherries by the river. She wants oranges on the hill. And so they stand there staring at one another, at the gift God has given to each of them. And they praise God?

But they are gifts to one another. Without the other, Adam or Eve begins to imagine that the purpose of this world is to feed his or her own tastes. By himself Adam sees the entire world as serving his body. He can taste, eat, and smell whatever he wants, whenever he wants. But with another who can choose, who can love, taste, feel, who experiences the world in a different way, his needs are limited. His body must now be in relationship with a body that is not his, a body that experiences the world in its own unique way. She must see and taste and experience the world through a body that is not hers. With the same capacities and freedom, the two of them together have to answer the question, "How will we live in this world?"

To be like God, Adam and Eve experience the goodness of this world through their bodies, bodies that cannot see and touch and feel everything at once. They are limited, only sensing the world from a very particular place. But their experience, their senses are also offerings. What they see and feel is always their own to be shared so that the other might see the world anew, again and again. Like a parent watching their child taste chocolate or oranges for the first time, the gift of another allows me to find joy in the mundane again and again. The gift of the body beside me is the proliferation of beauty in the everyday. Our bodies allow us to feel our world and to see its variances, its dangers, its pleasures, even as the body of another reminds us that our sight, our taste, our words cannot capture the fullness of the world we walk in.

Our bodied existence is a life of friendship, childhood, parenthood, family, and tribe. It is a life of fetching water and preparing meals. Each of these relationships brings intimacies and joys, belonging, and reminders of the gift that the world is not entirely as we see it. In a racial world this beauty, this intimacy, takes rings of love and beats them into shackles, held by one and binding the other. It is a relationship that determines what some bodies are for and ignores any experience but its own. The creation of the racial world does not learn; it teaches, it consumes, it uses, it mistakes love for hierarchy, order.

But love is not distance in God's life. Love is a presence in our bodies and a presence with us in the garden, in the world. To say that I love my son is to wash him when he is an infant, to listen to his cries and hear the frustration in one and the pain of the other. To love is to embrace him when he is a little lost. To love him is to hear his loping walk up the stairs, to smell oxtail soup and see his joy at the first taste of his favorite meal. Love is our bodies oriented toward one another in hope and faith, living with those we cannot know because they are not us. (As if we even know ourselves!) Through our bodies we participate with God's creation, living into God's image. To be made an image of God is to be in relationships that confront us with differences that are seen and felt. It is through our bodies that we come to know who God is and who we are—bound to God, bound to one another, and bound to this earth from which we came.

We are dirt, wet with Spirit. I am more than just a collection of cells. Who I am is tied to my body. My soul, the way I hope or mourn, what I love are never disconnected from my particular face, the way I experience the world. I am not who I am without *this* body. The story of Adam and Eve's creation out of the ground and out of one another and out of God is the image of this fundamental union of body and soul. Adam and Eve are created through and with the Spirit. Their material existence is not simply a biological process. If we think of God bending down into the dirt and gathering the clay together, God's Spirit breathes upon that earth in order to make something new. We are not just fleshly bodies or intellectual processes. What makes us human is this union of flesh and Spirit, a relationship to God that permeates our body. The only reason why Adam does not fall to pieces is because of the Spirit that holds him together. Like sand wet with ocean water, the atoms of our bodies hold together because of God's presence with us, holding us together. God perpetually wills us to exist. But what of Eve? The Spirit causes Adam to sleep and out of his rib forms Eve. Adam is the sand of Eve's existence, clay molded, pulled from and breathed into so that the two might be one, that the two, in their loving and binding and hoping, reflect the one.

They are earth and Spirit, created and uncreated wound into one. The grains of Adam and Eve's very lives are no longer the dry particles of sand that would perpetually fall from one another making only indiscriminate mounds. No, in the inbreathing of the Spirit the very breath of God saturates those grains, the moisture of God's life and love binding it to them so that they might bind to one another. Wet from God's words of institution, this dirt becomes clay and that clay becomes life.

The relationship of Adam and Eve to the land is not simply one of stewardship, of ruling over. Every time they tended a tree, dug a ditch, or plucked fruit from a tree they were reminded that they were not so different than that dirt or that tree. In a racial world, colonizers believed that the world existed to be subdued, that there were creatures so different from human beings that they should be packed onto boats or herded into pens. But the misperception was twofold. The colonizers thought life could be created and determined, but ignored just how fragile their lives were, just how much like the trees or the squirrels they were. We are all dust and breath.

We are like these other creatures. They're always a part of us, reminders that we are creatures too. We eat. We sleep. We make homes. We conceive new life. We are made from the ground and into the ground we will return.

We are like God. Eve's and Adam's lives—breathing, working, playing—testify to how God perpetually sustains and loves. To be human, to be made in the image of God, is to be in a relationship of difference and likeness (the *"father"* is not the *son*, the *son* is not *"father"*). The true depth of this likeness would come in incarnation. Jesus's life as divine and human revealed the nature of our humanity. We are dust held together by God's breath. There is no aspect of our life that is far from God because the same God who uttered us into existence is present with us, has identified with us in our humanity.

The aspects of my body, my skin, my lips, my hair, and the significance of my body in the world cannot be ignored for some deeper truth. These are beautiful aspects of who I am and who I was created to be. My flesh is as beautiful as my spirit. They reflect one another. In their unity I am like God. To hope for the death of race is not to diminish the beauty of my body, but to declare the fullness of its beauty.

The story of race reduces the entirety of who I am to my skin, to my hair, to my eyes or nose. I am a black-mixed man who loves soccer, gets nervous at parties and receptions. I am intensely loyal to a few friends, but generally keep to myself when I meet new people. I hold black history as my history, even if I grew up in a white suburb. I have a story that is more than race, even if race is an indelible part of my walk in this world. I am a whole person. I am *flesh*—history, relationships, tastes, desires. I am Spirit—hope, love, personality, intellect, joy. The story of race reduces me to my body and to a narrow, shallow story of what my body means.

I need to come back to the story of our beginnings because I need a story that helps me to understand my and my brother's differences, not simply ignore them. I need to see in these opening moments of humanity's existence a story of who we were created to be, without the specter of white supremacy rendering some bodies so visible and others so invisible. I need to return to this story so that I can see just how our relationships with one another, the meaning and purpose we sense about our lives together, are a display of a profound freedom, a freedom that is worked out through our bodies. The differences and similarities between men and women, what our bodies are for and what they are not for, these are the ways we confess who we are, how we live into God's image. We cannot find salvation with truer beliefs. We can only find our lives in God through bodied lives that reflect a freedom to love, to create, to tend for the sake of one another. We are not free when we seek sovereignty; we are free when we seek love, and love can only be seen in different bodies choosing one another. That is the story of our beginnings.

If I can reimagine Christianity in a racial world it would begin with telling the story of our beginnings. I would ask children to see their differences with wonder and awe. I would ask them to discover their sameness with curiosity. Like those books that let you take apart and combine different creatures' heads and bodies and feet, learning what it means to be made in the image of God begins with discovering the many ways this image could look, even as we wrestle with the truth that it cannot be whole without all of us in its pages.

Freedom is not sovereignty. When my first child, Caleb, was born I went to the mall for some film. I don't know why I hadn't packed more. I stepped off the escalator when I heard a baby cry. My head began to whip around and I had to quell an alien instinct to comfort that stranger's child. My world had changed. I was a father. This might seem a little obvious. I did not know how to be a father, but I knew that Caleb's life and needs were part of who I was. My life was now devoted to understanding this little life, learning about who he was and who he would become. There was now no such thing as a "me" without him.

One of the most profound lies about the creation of humanity is the idea that what makes us like God is a kind of sovereignty, a freedom from contingency and connection. When men justified the exclusion of women from education or certain occupations, they used language of dependency—that women were subject to their own bodies, subject to emotions, physically weaker. Somehow men were seen as being more "like" God because of a perceived independence, an ability to emotionally disconnect. They did not bear children and were not obviously limited by childbearing or nursing. When European explorers and colonizers first encountered indigenous peoples they commented on how the indigenous people seemed to be subject to nature, primitive, like animals. To be like God was to control and subdue the land. In this story of creation freedom meant sovereignty, independence—that certain differences were signs of who should and should not be able to determine their own life.

In our contemporary moment we can see how distorted the idea of freedom becomes when it is understood as sovereignty. The summers of 2014 and 2015 were punctuated by protests in Ferguson, Missouri. The first began in response to the death of Michael Brown, an eighteen-year-old African American who was shot by a police officer. His body was left in the street for hours after the incident and serious questions arose regarding why the police officer had initiated the encounter and whether or not the officer was actually in danger. This incident was one of many similar encounters between police and the people of Ferguson. Federal investigators would later outline a pattern of over-policing, designed less as service and more as a way of generating income. In the subsequent days, young people throughout Ferguson began to protest the lack of investigation. The protests intensified when police responded with militarized force, including body armor, snipers, and armored vehicles. A year later Ferguson would see another intensification of protests as the community marked the one-year anniversary of Michael Brown's murder.

This notion of sovereignty, of a freedom to possess, to be heard, to build, to speak, is not unique to police or avowed white supremacists. The violence in Ferguson displayed this myth writ large, that police officers' authority should not be challenged and, more specifically, certain bodies do not have the right to themselves. The contestation of Ferguson demonstrated what police valued, as armored cars and militarized police responded to words and sticks. The show of force was justified as necessary for protecting the community and the police. The danger to police officers' lives was difficult to see, but the challenge to their illusion of sovereignty was clear. As police unions respond to accusations of police brutality and over-policing, there is a presupposition among police that there is nothing they do not have a right to. Whether the bodies are black, native, or Latinx, the protests are speaking against the sense of autonomy among police, that their judgment is somehow not subject to the same prejudices and racial formations as the rest of the country. As police confront person after person, police brutality seems to become more intense and more deadly the more directly their authority and sovereignty is challenged.

"I'm just me." The idea of sovereignty isn't an easy idea for a mixed-race boy in America to resist, one who so often feels in between, feeling determined by ideas of black-and-white he can never quite fit into. As a boy, I clung to the mantra "I'm not black or white, I'm just me." I wanted the freedom to say who I was, apart from the ways that others would determine me. But then I read W. E. B. Du Bois's account of himself, "What does it feel like to be a problem?"[4] It was when I read his moment of recognition, that he was different than the others in his class, recognition that he was black in the eyes of so many people in his class, that I realized

---

4. W. E. B. Du Bois, *The Souls of Black Folk*.

I was part of the African American story. My freedom was not understanding myself apart from that story, but understanding that my dark body did work in the world, that it was seen in particular ways and I could not escape that fact. In discovering this story I found a freedom in needing the African American story in order to understand who I was.

For me, freedom was the risk of entering a community and a story in the middle, because I was always tethered to the story and formation of my white mother and family. Sovereignty is pretending those stories don't matter or have a claim on me. But in so many ways this was not really a risk. For others the idea of freedom is not simply the idea of being me. Their lives are, on a daily basis, circumscribed by ideas that other people have about them. They're limited by others' fears about them. They're limited by others' belief in their capacity. They're limited by socioeconomic realities and so they're never allowed to walk through the garden figuring out what fruit they would like to eat and where they would like to eat it. In this sense, their relationship to another has been overdetermined by someone who does not see them as being made in the image of God.

To say that freedom is a central aspect of who we are is not simply to say we can choose. To be free is to live in the world in such a way that we can taste and see the world and others in the world—their face, their village, their eyes, their language, all can speak to us. To be made as a union of flesh and spirit, in relationship and free, is to be made to live with God and one another. The power of our bodies lies in their limitations. Our senses help us to know and understand so much. But our bodies can only see and hold and know so much. Because of this, difference is always an opportunity to understand God, the world, others, and ourselves more deeply. Our bodies and their differences are not impediments to loving God. They are what make love, faith, and hope possible.

We are free for one another. So when God says, "Let us make them in our image, male and female" and tells them they can eat of any tree, that they are to name the animals, God does not make them sovereign, God gives mutuality. They must offer and receive. This freedom animates and orients their relationships and their enspirited bodies. This is not a freedom *from*. We often think of freedom as freedom from our parents, as freedom from tyranny or freedom of choice. Freedom from others making decisions for us, freedom from being bound to people we don't like, freedom from having our time or our vocations being overly determined.

Adam and Eve's freedom is freedom *for* one another, a life of *mutual* self-giving. If we do not have people we can share with and receive from, we are not truly free. Adam and Eve are free in community. In God's freedom, God wills toward another, even within God's own life. Lives are wrapped up within the life of God and in the life of one another.

Sometimes freedom is a limitation. To some, the ideas of being bound to another and freedom seem counterintuitive, even contradictory. And yet oftentimes the boundaries of our lives allow us to experience life more fully. When my children were young I would occasionally bring home a small gift, a GI Joe or transformer, maybe just a twenty-five-cent bouncy ball. Taking it from its wrappers they would shout with excitement, and the next week or two I would find it in amazing battles with dinosaurs or Legos. I would find it in a place of honor next to their pillow or on their dresser. On other occasions I would treat them to a morning at the toy store. "Okay boys," I would say, "ten dollars for each of you to get something fun at the toy store this morning!" We'd pile into the car and rumble off to the toy store. Along the way they would discuss all the possibilities and what each person had been wanting, and upon entering the store each would scamper to their chosen aisle. Arriving at the GI Joe aisle their eyes would light up as they took down the Snake Eyes action figure they had been talking about on the way. "How much is it?" they would ask. "7.99 plus tax, so you're good," and they would smile, but then something would inevitably catch their eye. In this case it was Snake Eyes with a motorcycle included for only 13.99. "It's only four dollars more!" Sticking to my guns I told them "no" and asked what was wrong with the thing they were so excited about in the car. "It's just not the same!"

For another hour we strolled through the store, the stress and dissatisfaction mounting until we finally returned to the original toy. My son begrudgingly handed over his $10 and we went home. Snake Eyes was played with for a while, but eventually I found him resting under a few books. "Why aren't you playing with your new toy?" I ask. "It's boring," he said. "I can't play with him without the motorcycle."

The freedom of God is not limitless choice. Freedom is the creativity and peace of creating new things with the trees, the people, the moments that are given to us. Because we are limited creatures, when we see freedom as unlimited choices, we can only create that freedom by determining what others are for (or not for), by determining what is mine and what you cannot have. My son had so much to choose from, only to become completely unhinged by the choices in front of him and unable to comprehend the choices that seemed too far out of reach for him. This freedom only led him to freedoms that he did not have but believed he should have had. This freedom only led him to a kind of bondage, a prison that allowed him to only look out upon the window to faraway fields of what he could not have, never seeing the possibilities of what was given to him. I believe he was free when, upon receiving this gift, he entered into an imaginative wonder where his action figure could miraculously play with Lego people and plastic dinosaurs. For days or weeks this simple toy was both a source of joy and a reminder that he was loved and valued. My children were free as they discovered new aspects of ordinary toys. They were free to enjoy one another.

The story of Eve and Adam is a story of freedom that begins in the reception of those goods that God gives to us and in the reception of ground that feeds us. Freedom is not all things that we can want or imagine. It is discovering the possibilities of our particular bodies, our particular relationships, our vocation as loving and being loved, of working and being worked upon.

What began with those few words by Du Bois became conversations with fellow black students and eventually visits to black churches with my Korean American girlfriend. I grew to find a home with folks in the Black Student Union at Duke Divinity School and mentors who told me my questions were important. The spirituals and gospel songs, theologies of liberation, the tensions between protest and accommodation, all of these various stories, various responses to the realities of race and racism helped me to see myself in new ways. I thought I was free when I held on so fiercely to the claim "I am just me." But I was never less free than when I resisted the story of my body told in the black community. To say that I am black, that I am white, is to receive the limitations and the possibilities of those communities, to discover God in my midst in new ways every day.

The idea of race is so pernicious because it is life stripped of color and shade and shadow. It takes the forms of our life and lets them remain while recasting the light to hide nuance, the complications of difference and likeness. Race names some differences as all-important, and submerges others as inconsequential. Race is a simple story told to describe an intricate world. But simple stories can never tell the truth, can never convey a world full of color. We are made in the image of a God whose life is relationship, whose life is difference and likeness and presence and love. The stories of our beginnings, of our bodies, will be the story of our love and our hope, for one another, for ourselves, and for our world.

3

Naked and Ashamed

My father died from cancer when I was seventeen. Diagnosed when I was fifteen, he had only been given three months to live. While it seemed sudden, the cancer had probably been growing in his colon for much, much longer. Who knows what the cause was? It could have been alcoholism, or stress, or the seemingly daily trips to McDonald's. But I was convinced it was fast food. By my early twenties I had begun to significantly curb how much fast food I ate. I avoided burgers and French fries (most days). But I didn't eat more fruits and vegetables or exercise any more or consider the possibility of my genes or stress. I was convinced my father's illness had a singular cause. Believing I understood the problem, I was less afraid of cancer, less afraid of facing the illness that took my dad. The delusion was comforting.

It does not take a lot to see just how broken our world is. Violence, selfishness, and utter disregard for one another's flourishing can be truly overwhelming. There are too many signs of our human brokenness, our refusal of God's life for us. Racism is one of these aspects of our society that we say is due to human sin. Early in my Christian walk I was told that when it really came down to it, racism was about focusing on the wrong thing. It was like eating fast food. We consume a food that is not good for us and it produces hatred or ignorance—that somehow, if we focus on good things we will be good people.

The solution was to ignore the difference, see people for the "content of their character," to parrot Dr. King. As much as I hoped this was true, I saw in my own life how intention is not enough. I was born in a racialized world. I would have to wrestle with my own bias, how the son of a black man could privilege white bodies and ideas. I would have to ask difficult questions about why ideas of beauty or intelligence seemed to be so racially coded in my own life and in America. I could not ignore how I saw these codes repeated in court cases and classrooms. I would have to wrestle with a history where dark bodies seemed to be perpetually demonized. The patterns of racial violence, indigenous genocide, Japanese internment, or black disenfranchisement seemed to never end. But even more, they seemed to reproduce even without individual complicity. I saw how I had been formed, how the currents of race somehow shaped and reshaped me. We don't need to have laws for separate and unequal schools because depressed housing prices and school funding tied to mortgage taxes do the work. We are fallen creatures.

The Fall is a cancer. Of course racism is a sin, but does this make the response any easier? To say simply that racism is a sin ignores the peculiar shape and rhythms of our world's condition. That somehow recognizing that it is contrary to God's intentions makes it easier to recognize and simply turn the other cheek. Sometimes it's said that racism is simply about individual intentions, a few bad apples, or that racism is not really about race at all—it is really about pride, greed, or selfishness. This is wishful thinking. Like believing my father's illness had a singular cause, I was delusional in my belief that I could change just one behavior and inoculate myself from the possibility of cancer in my body.

In many ways the Fall is like cancer. Our bodies are made of cells. The cells divide according to a particular pattern given how they function in the body. They function within a beautiful ecology of mutuality. Cancer is growth without mutuality. It is the proliferation of life unto death, drawing blood and nutrients, and dividing and dividing until it blocks the colon or fills your lungs with tumors of stolen life. It is not contagious, so it cannot find life outside the body, but it grows nonetheless, consuming its host until both cease to function. It is attributable to the foods that we eat, to the air that we breathe. Its likelihood increases when we are exposed to high levels of the very technologies and chemicals we create to make our lives easier, or the choices of others dropped as bombs, or waste, or unregulated technologies.

And so cancer lies like a sleeping potentiality in every one of us, our bodies just waiting for a trigger or a food or a combination of all these things to become a disease in our bodies and turn life against itself. And perhaps racism is uniquely like cancer. Racism is latent in us all because we are all free; we have the capacity to divide and subdivide, to see difference and name those differences. We even have the power to direct resources toward us or to others depending on the power our place in this ecosystem provides us. Racism is like cancer because our likeness to God—our capacity to name, to care for, to choose, to be in relation to another who is not us, the necessity for another—is rendered in such a way that dark bodies are perpetually used, plundered, and raped in order to serve the needs of the one who names.

Racism is like a cancer because it takes the life of the other and transforms mutuality into enslavement, a necessity where one must always serve the other, where one's identity as master is dependent on another's identity as slave.

If we are going to account for the death of race in our lives and in our society we must see its beginnings in our fall. We do not wish cancer away. We cannot wish race away. Race is the contemporary incarnation of an old and wicked word. To find a new way we need to return to the story of our beginnings, to see how difference becomes distortion and these differences are hewn into fortresses, structures of human civilization that destroy so that some may live. To see the possibility of freedom, we must see the contours of our bondage.

Retelling the story of our fall. Sick of the "What are you?" question, I told people "I am just me, alright?!" That's what I wanted. To be a person who could name myself, whose identity was determined by my words and actions. Maybe that is a uniquely American sentiment, but it seems like so much of the violence and dissension in human history comes from such a simple contestation. The violence we hurl at one another is a manifestation of our wish for this to be true rather than an assertion of what is. We are all bound to one another. My life and history are tied up in the history of my mother and my brother and my father. We can't untangle ourselves from each other or each other's histories.

When I come back to the story of humanity's fall I still see some of the pride and hubris I was taught to see when I was a young Christian. Adam and Eve desire to be like God and seek something that is not meant for them. They violate God's law, God's justice. But even more than in the story of the Fall I see our propensity to mistake freedom for individuality. I see us estranged from our bodies, hiding the very aspects of ourselves that make us different than one another. We are naked and ashamed of our difference. When I return to Genesis and read of Adam, of Eve, I discover myself in new and terrifying ways. Somehow the more we see, the less we understand. But this was even harder when I had to talk to my children about why there is so much evil in the world. They hear news of black men and women shot by police who are supposed to protect them. In Social Studies they learn of slavery and internment and the legacies of patriarchy. When my children ask me how things got this way, I go back to the beginning, to the story of our creation and our fall, how the cancer began.

> Now the serpent was more crafty than any other wild animal that the Lord God had made. He said to the woman, "Did God say, 'You shall not eat from any tree in the garden'?" The woman said to the serpent, "We may eat of the fruit of the trees in the garden; but God said, 'You shall not eat of the fruit of the tree that is in the middle of the garden, nor shall you touch it, or you shall die.'" But the serpent said to the woman, "You will not die; for God knows that when you eat of it your eyes will be opened, and you will be like God, knowing good and evil." So when the woman saw that the tree was good for food, and that it was a delight to the eyes, and that the tree was to be desired to make one wise, she took of its fruit and ate; and she also gave some to her husband, who was with her, and he ate. Then the eyes of both were opened, and they knew that they were naked; and they sewed fig leaves together and made loincloths for themselves. (Genesis 3:1–7)

When God created us, God created us to be like God. God wanted us to love and to be loved. But when you love someone you have to choose them. You have to choose them in the big things and in the small things. To love someone you have to see how they are like you and how they are not like you, and you have to see how their differences are gifts, ways of helping you to see yourself and God and the world in new ways. We were made like fountains that are always being filled by a stream of living water and pouring out into the other fountains around us. We are always being filled and we are always pouring out. That's what it means to be made in God's image.

God puts us in the garden with one another, with creatures, and with two trees—the Tree of Life and the Tree of the Knowledge of Good and Evil. Our lives are made whole in these differences. Difference is the opportunity to choose one another and to choose God. If we each desire something different, our morning ritual requires recognition of another, and in that seeing we must put our needs or desires into conversation with the other. In that small decision we must choose the other. In that moment we have an opportunity be free, to love. These small moments of freedom accumulate to become friendships or marriages, com-munities, even nations, as groups of people gather toward one another for each other. We choose this freedom by loving the one who is not us.

In the garden we walk by these two trees every day. God did not hide the tree away or place it behind impenetrable walls. It grew among the many other trees. It bore fruit and grew like any other and in this way it stood before Adam and Eve, before us as a mark of their freedom. We could choose *not* to eat and in not eating we would confess God as our creator, the one whom we cannot be without. We love the tree by not hacking it down to see what the insides look like. We honor the difference and the mystery of God when we acknowledge that the Tree of the Knowledge of Good and Evil is not intended to nourish us like other trees do.

But in our freedom we, Eve and Adam, did not rest in this relationship. We did not enjoy the trees given to us. Much has been made of Adam and Eve's first bite of the fruit of the Tree of the Knowledge of Good and Evil, of whether Eve or Adam was *truly* at fault. But in this tragic moment they both sought something beyond what they had been given. In the Tree of the Knowledge of Good and Evil, they both sought an unlimited life. We take, cut, tear, beat, consume, enslave what we believe is ours to know. Our eating was the slightest tilt of that beautiful freedom, away from God, and away from one another.[1]

In our disobedience a new world opened up. We could see. The serpent was not lying in some respects; we human beings continued to breathe and think and love. But something had changed. Scripture says that upon eating the fruit, Adam and Eve "saw that they were naked and were ashamed." Our bodies did not transform into some grotesque shape as soon as we tasted the fruit. No, with this new knowledge we could no longer see the blessed significance of our bodies, of our lives together. The knowledge we gained drove us into hiding, hiding our bodies from one another and hiding ourselves from God. We were terrified by a true knowledge of our *in*capacity. But this knowledge did not lead us to cry out, to see ourselves truthfully. This new knowledge and our transgression were knit into our very lives and bodies. As we look at one another and the world around us, our knowledge makes us blind.

---

1. Some Christians have suggested that Adam and Eve's eating of the fruit was a prideful act of willful disobedience that required punishment while still others have suggested that the eating was an ignorant, childlike disobedience that had tragic consequences. But it could be said that Adam and Eve, in their eating, desired something beyond the limits God gave them. In their eating they took for themselves a knowledge that they could not handle, that exceeded their capacities.

Yet, Adam and Eve remained God's children, unique creatures with whom God desired to dwell, to love and be loved by. In this moment we did not lose the image of God. God did not withhold God's animating Spirit and love toward us, but something changed nonetheless. In the Fall our likeness to God became a cancerous freedom, an all-consuming, death-bound life, slowly spreading in Adam and Eve and in us.

The Fall is a social system. Our world is now marked irrevocably by our refusal of communion with God, so often mistaking our own machinations as holy and divine. And like a cancer, this distortion of the *image of God* divides, becoming a pattern of disorder, paving over transgression with ignorance, denial, or fear. These refusals become social, ecosystems where bodies and land exist to make another person's life possible. We become like fountains no longer filled by streams, pouring out into one another. We become cesspools, stagnant water where bacteria breed. When the water ran, there was life. Where it grows still, death flourishes.

We are not autonomous individuals. We are formed by a society's assumptions, by the neighborhoods we grow up in, by the ways people see us, and the way we see them. These various aspects of a social system work like a stream flowing through mountains and hills, slowly cutting curving paths through the earth. These forces shape us, even when we are resisting.

No longer bone of my bone, flesh of my flesh. When I read accounts of the Fall and look up into the world I begin to see these patterns of unfaithfulness in my own life, in the assumptions that were slowly formed in me, in relationships, in our bodies, in our very ideas of freedom and love.

Adam and Eve were "bone of bone and flesh of flesh." We inhabit God's image in the midst of deep and essential relationships with others, with the land, and with God. But when God confronted Adam, Adam blamed Eve, and Eve blamed the serpent. Adam didn't want to be bone of my bone, flesh of my flesh. He wanted to be autonomous, alone. Adam imagined that his righteousness and his identity could be understood apart from Eve, the one who shared his very body. Similarly, Eve imagined her life apart from the serpent, this creature of the ground that dwelled in the land given to them.

I don't want to be seen as every other man when confronted by the realities of sexual harassment or sexism. I don't want to be seen as the light-skin guy when we have conversations about the histories of colorism, the valuing of light skin over dark, in the black community.

My desire to be seen as an individual is bound to a certain presumption that if you looked at my life, on its own, you'd see something more righteous than another's. But this requires a pretty big leap for me. This leap requires me to ignore all of the ways my ideas weren't challenged in class while the woman next to me couldn't make the slightest comment without it being dismissed or corrected. This assertion of independence would require me to ignore the times I did not risk speaking up when I heard men harass or catcall a woman on the street, or ignore the truth that I live on stolen land, or how death rates, education, and poverty are so inextricably bound to race. "But that's not my job," some might say. In the end, belief in my individuality is really about freeing myself from responsibility to risk something for someone else, to see their struggles and burdens as my own.

This is one of the most fiendish symptoms of our fall. We

believe that we are whole without an other. Our justification, or our presumed innocence then gets mapped onto the very differences God gave us to see our limitations. Adam claimed his identity by *not* being Eve. Eve asserted herself by *not* being with the serpent. The relationship is not severed. It is warped, shifted ever so slightly so that relationship does not create one flesh. Now relationships and differences exist to display what I am and what I am not. Adam needs Eve to be less so that he can claim to be more.

I sometimes wonder if that seeming instantiation of hierarchy—"Your husband will rule over you"—was less about hierarchy and more God's attempt to say, "You cannot be without one another, even if it is broken and uneven." That Adam was "now" to rule over Eve suggests a shift in the structure of this relationship. In creation the fullest expression of the image of God was the mutuality of the two, two persons and one humanity. But in the Fall, Adam and Eve were exiled into a relationship of powers and submissions, submissions that the male writers of these texts seemed to see so easily.

The lie of our independence. Death enters the world and bares itself in the patterns of our lives together, in the miraculous and the mundane. In every relationship, whether to the land under our feet or the wonder of new life, we see the symptoms of this cancer growing, and God's commands that seem to never let us fall into an illusion of independence.

In fallen relationships to one another, and then to the land, Adam and Eve were reminded of the necessity that marked their lives with one another, with God, and with the land. This ground that gave birth to Adam's body would be a mystery to him. He would toil and struggle to feed, and in another moment pain or storm will fall, leaving them with nothing. That land would remind them again and again of what they did not know and yet were always in need of. Their relationship with one another and with the land was not a relationship of sovereignty. Land was not simply origin and sustenance. The land was part of who they were; it signified their beginning and end with God. Working the land, burying the dead, welcoming new life into the world were moments where they participated in God's life and work, even within their limitations.

In childbirth, Eve's creative capacity, her body as a space of life holding within it something that was both intimately tied to her and yet different from her, was a sign of God's own creative act and her own beginnings in Adam's body. But her creative capacity would no longer be the ease of sleep. She would feel her body. The rhythms of her life would be oriented around this creative possibility reminding her of her limitation, of her own beginnings, of the gift and struggle that is conception and birth. Those who love her would have to wait with her; would have to bear her life in their own ways. The community now shared in this pain.

When I read about humanity's fall I am not simply reading about two individuals who failed to obey a rule and must now endure punishment. The working of the land and the pain of childbirth are not specific to genders—as though women did not farm and work the land, or a man cannot be anguished as he gasps and holds and sighs with the woman in his life during childbirth, or lies exhausted from constant feedings and changes in a home with newborns. God's words to Adam and Eve are indicators of how our communal life is bound to the bodies we inhabit. The toil of this fallen condition is a shared state of being even as each person experiences it in unique ways. And yet, the burden of this fallen state is not one person's alone. We all bear one another's burden of living in this new world.

Race is a tragic incarnation of this fallen transformation of relationship. The land becomes a resource to be manipulated and consumed. The totality of our personhood is reduced to differences of skin and hair and eyes. Women's bodies become read as weak and their identities reduced to reproduction. Even the intimacy of sex, that profound display of mutual self-giving and pleasure, becomes debased as white colonizers and slave masters routinely rape black and indigenous women. The new lives born of these violent encounters are made into slaves themselves. Race is not simply about people who are judgmental or focus too much on differences. Race is a social system that establishes the personhood of one people through the dehumanization of others.

Death enters the world. We see this dehumanization and death emerge in Adam and Eve's bodies. While their lives did not immediately cease upon eating the fruit, their bodies underwent a change. Their exile from the garden was an exile from a certain communion, an intimacy within God's life that replenished the water of their lives. This distance would seep into our very bones. No longer communing with God, their distance now exposed them to a dry desert with their bodies of clay and Spirit far from living water. Our immortality does not belong to us—it is perpetually given. Adam and Eve drew away from the source of their life and fell again into nonbeing. We see this truth when we bury those we love and say, "from dust to dust." Our bodies return to the ground to become earth again.

While Adam and Eve remained alive, they woke up each morning, foraged for food, cared for the land, tried to survive by gathering wood and water. Their bodies were caught in the gap, the irrevocable distance that was spawned in the eating of the tree of the knowledge of good and evil. The union of flesh and Spirit, of clay enlivened by God's very breath, now expressed its distance in its decay, in its slow and inevitable movement toward death and their bodies' return to dust. We are estranged from ourselves, every day trying to find some semblance of wholeness and life, grasping at tree branches or faint assertions of our innocence and another's guilt to assuage the feeling that we are not in control of our lives, our bodies.

And so to somehow feel alive, to resist the visceral reminders that our bodies are so fragile, so contingent, we have to kill or enslave or dominate in order to find a shadow of life for ourselves. We have built tents and castles and towers and towns and tribes. What I've come to see is that the death of my body isn't the only kind of death that multiplies in the moribund waters of our fallen lives. We render others unseen, invisible, little more than animals, because to acknowledge them is to acknowledge the lie that is our life. American slave society was kept alive well after the Civil War through this insidious manipulation. Poor white men and women, believing their white bodies superior to black bodies, failed to see just how racism subjugated them to continual poverty. While rich plantation owners retained their land after the war, poor whites continued to toil in dead-end towns with subpar schools, reluctant to join with black men and women to struggle for a more equitable society. The death of race marks us all.

Sovereignty is a cancerous freedom. But above all in Adam and Eve's disobedience their freedom turned upon themselves and against one another. Who they believed themselves to be could only be constituted through twisted processes of differentiation and violent subjugation. This distortion of freedom is a kind of sovereignty, an utter freedom from others that was tragically expressed almost immediately after their expulsion from Eden as their children's attempts to worship became twisted into fits of jealousy.

Abel and Cain, the two sons of Adam and Eve, made offerings to God, but God found only Abel's pleasing (Genesis 4:1–16). In the midst of Cain's lack he sought a righteousness, a freedom, by erasing his brother's presence, creating his own faithfulness, his own way to enter into God's presence. But we are all Cain, building edifices of "I am" upon broken stones of what others are not. Freedom, the capacity to choose, to name, to build, to create, is trapped within a desperate and perpetually failing attempt to build ourselves, to create the means to live and call ourselves whole.

The disorientation of freedom was perhaps most clearly seen in humanity's attempt to build a tower that could reach God (Genesis 11:1–9). Their powers of intellect and capacity to manipulate creation for their purposes coalesced not in worship of God or rest in their own createdness. Babel rose, aspiring to divine heights, built with stones torn and cut from mountains by laborers shorn from families.

Here we find the earliest residue of evil, spreading now as economics, as urban and suburban, as walls and insiders and outsiders. Evil is a creation that grows against God's purposes, that is violent and consuming in its attempt to assert itself over against God and orient all relationships toward itself, to be a god in the world. While it is tempting to suggest that evil is fundamentally an absence, that it has no power and no existence in itself, too many of us have seen evil in explicit and active ways. The deathly consequences of race and patriarchy are not absence. They are not imagined. They wreak havoc in our bodies and lives.

Cancer grows uncontrollably in the body, overtaking every function meant to uphold its life until organs are overwhelmed, like the malevolence of a man leading a nation toward utter and brutal violence against his neighbor. The distortion of human life and possibilities, the misuse of land, seem oftentimes senseless or the consequence of a God who can do little, or worse, simply chooses not to. But evil is neither the true center of our bodily lives nor a cruel instrument God uses to draw us back into God's presence.

No, evil is the infection that grows in the stagnant water, in the womb with the lifeless child that slowly overtakes the body of the mother and the child. It does not have its own life, but feeds on the death of others—until a fever, a cough, or chills make the infection's presence known. Evil does not remain the bad choices of one or another. This evil metastasizes; it winds its ways into the very structures of daily life until it is ordinary. Evil is the air we breathe. We do not question why we have slaves or why people in "that" country deserve to die in war and we should remain unharmed. Poverty becomes simply a social marker for a lack of ambition; wealth becomes a sign of hard work. From such a small seed, from an individual refusal, evil becomes incarnate, wrapped in skins of good business sense or supply and demand or "reasonable force." In the Fall, some must be slaves for us to be fed or must die in order for us to feel safe.

We exist in the mire of our refusal, sensing the distance, but seeking to fill the distance with deadly machinations and vain endeavors. This gap is about the stories that were woven into the Christianity of our so-called Western world. It is a story of chosenness and truth, of the individual and progress. America's story was a Christian story, written in bodies of black and white.

When I came to Christ and was told the story of the Fall, I was told it was a consequence of individual decisions and that it was my decision to repent, to follow Christ in order to escape the individual consequences of this fallen condition. But in Scripture the consequences of the Fall seem to rarely be individual. The consequences of humanity's refusal to see themselves with God cascade, dividing exponentially—Cain and Abel, the Tower of Babel, enslavement and enslaving others, greed, imperial domination, sickness, disease. The desire to be free from one another, the desire to determine one's own existence, are not solitary inclinations. Human sinfulness is a condition of our bodies turned *us* and *them* and *not me*. Our bodies are the ground of our love and our refusals.

We live as fallen bodies. Through our bodily lives we come to know the world, to discern and create meaning through symbols and rituals. Through our bodies we recognize what is not like us, or what is possible for us. Our culture, our identities, are the smells of Easter meals or the song that causes us all to sway just a little. It is the inside jokes and the glances at the one woman who looks like me in a sea of strange faces, and she is home to me. The beliefs about what we should do together (build a tower, for instance) or not do (do not marry a non-Jew)—form our society and shape what we understand to be faithful or unfaithful. Our bodies are a language, a kind of word that we speak and we hear. From simple articles of clothing, like a suit or a flowered skirt, to a tattoo or a certain kind of walk, all of these everyday things are part of the ways we speak with our bodies.

A word has meaning because of the relations of the letters or sounds. The word *peace* has meaning. You see it and immediately make an association, perhaps even a moment in your life or a hope for a nation. Each letter on its own corresponds to a sound, but the letters themselves do not convey the meaning. The lines and curves, visual signs, convey meaning when they are in relationship to one another, when they are aligned with one another in a particular order. It is their difference that makes this meaning possible and allows for meaning to come from a different order of letters. But what happens when these letters become stretched or disordered?

p   *e*   *a*   *c*   *e*

We can still discern the meaning of the word. But perhaps you felt the gap a bit more. You couldn't quite take in the whole word at first glance. The relationship between the "bodies" of each letter has become strained.

But imagine your body is a letter or, for example, a people from the valley of the Columbia River, and you come to believe the totality of the word *peace* can actually be found in your particular body, the *a* for instance. So the word looks like this:

p   *e*   *a*   *c*   *e*

To find some semblance of freedom, some people exercise what limited power they have to subjugate the bodies around them, pushing them off the page, rendering their bodies so inconsequential that their presence on the page is barely noticed, or is seen as only a blemish on an otherwise clean surface. In the Fall some bodies become marginalized or centered, read as more or less significant, ugly or beautiful to our communities.

These disordered determinations build up over time as they take root in our social bodies. This cancer feeds on the holy and the profane, using relation and war alike to kill. Frederick Douglass called American Christianity a "slaveholding religion," where "[t]he slave prison and the church stand near each other.[2] The clanking of fetters and the rattling of chains in the prison, and the pious psalm and solemn prayer in the church, may be heard at the same time. The dealers in the bodies and souls of men erect their stand in the presence of the pulpit, and they mutually help each other."[3] Slaveholders created economic and social capital that profited from slavery. This system was built upon a belief that slavery and racial classification was the order of things, that some bodies were meant to be used and others were meant to be users.

In this system the black female body was subjugated to rape (by white men for power, by other slaves for production of new bodies). It was pressed into domestic service, feeding, nursing, and caring for her children and the master's children—only to have them torn away or become her master when they learned America's lessons thoroughly. Every aspect of our bodily life was measured, weighed, valued, or devalued. It was a bell that would not cease to ring even as the Civil War ended. Race is the systemic tumor of the Fall—many small parts and movements each functioning with a singular purpose. That was slaveholding society—the gods

2. Frederick Douglass, "Narrative of the Life of Frederick Douglass, An American Slave." in African American Religious History: A Documentary Witness. Milton Sernett, ed. (Durham, NC: Duke, 1999), 107.
3. Ibid.

white men worshiped, cotton plantations in the South and shirt factories in the North, black codes and red lines—all pulling together.

Race and gender and our fallen condition. One night my wife and I attended a dinner with other families, mostly Korean American. We were all talking and laughing, and when it was time to get dinner ready the women, one by one, got up and began to find things to do in the kitchen. Meanwhile the men remained in the family room watching the game, telling stories about work or sports. My wife initially resisted the obvious division of labor that was unfolding. She stayed in the family room and continued her conversation, completely aware of the fact that she was the only woman left in the room.

I got up and went to the kitchen to get something to drink and found the women talking about their children, challenges in home and work life. I ended up staying and talking about raising children, the challenges of the waddling children and the transition from two to three children. Eventually, my wife joined me in the kitchen and, together, we helped to get dinner ready talking with the other wives.

Race is only the most recent of humanity's attempts to maintain an illusion of sovereignty. In our fallen condition women's bodies have been made ever present and utterly used, the productivity of their bodies rendered so natural to them that they were little more than pretty horses or strong oxen. Their individuality is stripped from them as men seek to articulate their identity over and against—seeking to make true the lie of male independence and superiority. I guess it should not come as a surprise, but we have not grappled with the death that men have wreaked upon women (and other men, for that matter). Myths of masculinity justified rendering women's bodies and lives perpetually inferior to men's bodies and lives. In these moments the gift of sexual intimacy, the mutuality of hearing and listening, giving and receiving turned into a violent consumption, a demonic theft grounded only in male desire to be free without limitation. In the modern world the myth of masculinity becomes infused with a racial imagination and utterly reshapes the world.

A society is never singular and homogenous, but rather constituted by the interrelationships, tensions, and unions of a multiplicity of cultures over time. Within this society groups and individuals can occupy a variety of positions within multiple cultures or identities. My identity is constituted by a myriad of intersecting claims and stories. And each of these claims is part of a larger story, a story of what it means to belong, to be American.

That night with our friends, my identity was not static. My maleness and my wife's femaleness did not explicitly dictate who should be in one room and who should be in another, as if the roles were somehow knit into our DNA. But there was a story that seemed to press in on everyone in that house, a story about who cooks, who attends to the lives of the children, who is free to rest when there is still work to do. In that moment my wife and I had to negotiate these implicit meanings ascribed to our bodies and what those meanings meant for what we did in that moment. My wife stayed and talked sports with the husbands, resisting the idea that her femaleness meant she needed to leave her seat on the couch, or the conversation. I was resisting the implication that I would not have something to contribute in the kitchen or the conversation about our children. Gail and I were navigating our identities and the subtle presumption this cultural space made about how we ought to live in that moment.

Among these people who have been marked by challenges of inclusion and belonging their whole lives, there nonetheless remained patterns of distinction within their Korean American culture regarding roles of men and women. As Gail and I navigated that cultural space, we were navigating what it meant to be a man, a woman, a Korean American, a black man in an Asian American space. All of these stories were intersecting in this moment, pressing claims on everyone present, though in various ways.

The consequences of the Fall are systemic. Race is the echo of an ancient aspect of our human existence. It is the word that encapsulates a particular people's belief in their own sovereignty and the tragic circumstances that allow them to wield that belief upon the world. The Fall is not a loss of image. The Fall is an evil that grows in the belief that we can be who we are without the "other." It is our constant effort to resist the inevitable evidence of our interdependence.

I would love to be able to say that because my father was black I was somehow free from this cancer, this proliferation of a false life that strangles everything within reach. But the reality is that I grew up listening to my mother and my father complain about people who didn't speak real English, who refused to pull themselves up by their bootstraps. My clinging to being mixed was as much about my own sense of alienation from the black community and a formation that saw that history as something different from my own. I was young, but with the awareness of my own history and my body's presence within that history, I had to begin to recognize the ways in which race formed me to believe that I could be "me" without "them." The cancer is everywhere.

The consequences of the Fall are not simply about our individual souls, our selfish desires, or the ways we misuse creation around us. The consequences of the Fall are systemic. They are policies and procedures. They are redlined housing districts. They are GI college bills, and black codes, and the war on drugs. They are immigration policies and school districts. But they are also images of All-Americanness, of who is beautiful and who is not, of implicit lessons about who can be trusted and who should be suspected that permeate even the fairest of policies.

The story of race is the story of painting guilt upon the dark bodies of the world. We want to be free, but we cannot imagine our freedom without forcing another's bondage. We cannot see another's freedom without recoiling from the supposed limitations it might mean for us. Like Adam and Eve, we can only imagine our freedom apart from one another, through the guilt of someone, anyone who is not us. The story of race is the story of painting that guilt upon the dark bodies of the world, imagining the world where all things can be consumed, where there is no limit. The story of race is the story of the American Dream, a sordid, wicked independence built upon dark bodies.

Cancer really is an insidious disease. It takes life and turns it against itself. The disease permeates our every bodily function so thoroughly that it is almost impossible to find the source once it has progressed. And like so many diseases, we seem to treat one only to find another manifestation, or another food, or another additive, or another technology that seems to contribute to the disease's continued existence.

The death of race is a disease with roots in our very earliest refusals of life with God. How I describe what is wrong has everything to do with how I treat the disease. I can't say that overcoming race is about being nice or ignoring difference any more than I can say my father's cancer could have been avoided by not eating at McDonald's. If we are to recognize the salvation that has come in Christ, we must see rightly the disease he came to cure.

4

This Is My Body, Born for You

My early Christian testimony would emphasize my loneliness, my insecurity and how, in Jesus, I found a home and a community. I found a freedom to speak. But I found that bondage was so much more than my insecurities or sinful desires. As I lived into what it meant to be a black man, I came to see and feel the bondage of America's racial cancer. As I walked life with Gail, I saw the chains of patriarchy continually winding themselves around her, trying to choke out her calling, close the doors to her gifts.

I was confronted with the legacy and enduring realities of bondage that were physical and spiritual and social. As I began to speak from the space of my black body I found my community began to shift. As a black Christian, a person of color, I came to understand that believing my body or my voice matters is, oftentimes, a sheer act of faith. Our lives are not lofty, abstract ideas. Bodied lives are groggy mornings, spoonfuls of cereal, quick glances at fellow pedestrians wondering if it is okay to let your eyes linger on theirs. Our lives are joy at finding a handful of people who love the same book that gave us hope, or who can't help moving their hips the same way when *that* song begins on the radio. Our lives are fights for dignity and wholeness and relationship in the midst of the daily, mundane rituals of life.

And alongside this we have to live and work in the midst of what we do not know. A bodied person carries their lack of knowledge, their mistakes, their overcoming with them; and these stories shape how they see themselves, their world, and what faithfulness could begin to look like. But in the face of this world's evils that are both extraordinary and mundane, in the midst of my seeming powerlessness, the heart of my Christian confession is that God is not far from me, or you. And this presence is liberating and redemptive.

I learned this from black preachers who proclaimed hope and constant reminders that our God is able. I was enveloped in the history of a people who kept running or sitting or marching because they knew God had made them more than what white men and women had spoken about them. It is a presence that makes us whole. God desires my freedom and my flourishing, and this flourishing is intended for *this* body, fearfully and wonderfully made.

In the midst of our fallen state, the death of race is ubiquitous. It touches everything and everyone. In the face of such an overwhelming reality we hope for a redemption that is clear, a savior who can overcome our enslavement in unequivocal terms. And yet, when we look at the stories of God's people we see redemptions that are ambiguous, at best. God's people interpret these promises imperfectly, in fits and starts. We see people chosen to speak who seem to have their own baggage, who seem to choose the wrong action at the wrong time. This is what it means to live in the waters of our sinful world. And yet, God comes for us. Despite our condition, despite the varying bondages and transgressions, God does not leave us alone. God redeems us by coming near.

God comes for us in the water. The story of race is the story of our fallen and fragmented condition. It is a confusion of our language, a misreading of what our capacity to build and create is for. Our racial world is not terribly far from the fragmentation of the world in Genesis 11, a world similarly confused and broken by man's (and I do mean *man's*) hubris. In Genesis 11, humanity thought they could reach God by building a tower, again transforming the land God gave them in order to determine who they were, to display their sovereignty rather than their createdness. In response, God confused their language and scattered humanity.

Race seeks to clarify the significances of our bodies. It is the creation of the European and a symptom of humanity's constant struggle with what it does not and cannot know. Uncertainty and ambiguity are part of what it means to be human, flesh and Spirit. Life will always be ambiguous because our bodies are always bound to a place and a story. Our motives and hopes and anger and desire are often as much of a mystery to us as they are to others. As bodied people we have to navigate the significance (or insignificance) that is attributed to our genealogy or our tribe, our gender, or our perceived (dis)ability. A person has to sometimes overcome the utter invisibility of their voice or their face in spaces of power and authority.

Like race, the tale of the tower of Babel is an account of human difference. It is a glimpse of how humanity tries to find meaning in the midst of a world that is overwhelming. Babel is about just how fearful we are of difference, of our difference with God, with one another. While we try to overcome difference, God presses difference back into us.

And God builds something new in the rubble of our fallen towers. In the very next chapter of Genesis, God called Abram and Sarai to become God's people. In the midst of this confusion God says to them, "Go from your country and your kindred and your father's house to the land I will show you, I will make of you a great nation" (Genesis 12:1–2). God becomes enfleshed, present, with a new people. God identifies with us. God lives in the world with us through a people who eat and herd and pray and sing. God has a tent, a place to sleep. A space the people point to and say, "Because God is there, we know who we are and who we ought to be." God answers the confusion of our fallen world by plucking two grains of sand and breathing them into a new people. God becomes a bodied identity, a culture, embedded in their language and as their way of life.

Abram and Sarai are bodies of God's redemption. Theirs was a life of fear and waiting and wandering. Each day they had to remind themselves of the promise God had given to them. They were promised to be the beginning of great nations. But Sarai was barren. Their names would be remembered, but they had no land. Their lives were alternating signs of God's miraculous power and our constant failings. But the story of God's life with us is the story of God answering death with presence, redeeming us, again and again, with people who have histories and families and fathers and mothers.

In so many ways, the story of Abram and Sarai is a reminder that God redeems us with bodies. Jesus sat with his disciples the night before he was crucified and said, "Take, eat; this is my body" (Matthew 26:26). God's redemption is always a bodied redemption, a redemption that takes up our everyday lives so that our everyday lives can be free. There is no redemption without God's presence.

The Christian story is that the Word becomes flesh. The Word is redemptive body, God fully immersing God's self into our fallen story, like putting a clean cloth in a tainted pool, hoping the cloth will cleanse the pool. This redemption does not only have our souls at its center, hoping our bodies will follow or at least be beaten into submission. A bodied redemption is about our flesh and our Spirit, the totality of who we are. A bodied redemption is risky because its end is the possibility of our freedom—a freedom to love and be with. This kind of redemption cannot be coerced or triggered through any machination, divine or otherwise. How can you make someone love you? How can we manipulate our tastes to crave what is best for us or willingly sacrifice what we enjoy so another can feel even the most basic nourishment?

Redemption is presence. From the very beginning of our resistance, God intervenes not with fiats, but with presence. God identifies with us. As Abel lay dead, Cain standing over him, blood still dripping from the rock, God sends Cain into the wilderness, but not from God's presence. As Babel falls and the peoples' tongues seize up with strange sounds, redemption is bound up in their stunted speech. They are given a gift of unknowing so that they might encounter difference again, and live into the faint promise of the *image of God* that was still God's intention.

God is present in the promise to Abram and Sarai; God's redeeming work became incarnate through the bodies of these two, identifying with them and the tribe they would become. Their story was a broken story, a story of faithfulness and unfaithfulness in the face of uncertainty. Trying to determine the uncertainty in their life, they would subject

69

another's body to use and production, employing a powerless Hagar's body to an ill-formed plan to be faithful. But even here, meeting Hagar in the wilderness, God's presence is reassuring and confounding. God is with those who possess power in such different quantities. God does not cease to press us or shelter us. Hagar returns to Abram and Sarai, an unholy family held together and confronted each morning with infidelity and betrayal. God's promise to all of them is fraught with ambivalence and faraway horizons. Whether Cain or Abram and Sarai, we live into God's life imperfectly, wounded and wounding.

Our failures are so often not just our own. We exile and abuse in the name of God, in the name of a homeland we are seeking. We are the ones whose bodies are bruised and beaten in the name of another people's faithfulness, crying out to be heard by God. Whether in the bodies and lives of women subjected to the terror of male power or to a nation that gives itself over to idols, Israel's God redeems through the curious body, the foreign woman, the prostitute, the prophet, the foreign king, a teenage girl in a poor, colonized town. God redeems by coming near.

Israel's life and law is a responsive presence to a God who has abided and is abiding. Our fallen condition is not fundamentally a spiritual state of being. In the fall our bodies and lives become entangled in the tumors of our deluded longing to order our world, determine our bodies and relationships. We are immersed in the wake of the world that has been made around us, and the perpetual word that our bodies are not enough, that our words do not count, that we were made to entertain or to be jailed, but little else.

When I read Scripture I do not see a God that simply declares forgiveness or measures justice with declarations of good or bad, punish or do not punish. I do not see a God who simply utters words without enfleshing them, without a presence that makes that word known and felt, that turns water into wine and makes bread pour from near-empty baskets. Our racial world is a world where our bodies have been measured, cut and stacked, brick-by-brick in a destructive naming. Like the men who sought to be like God and build a tower, men built civilizations with other human beings, hewing them one atop the other, with the belief that the white body ought to be free, to live without restraint. But just as the calling of Abram and Sarai follows the story of Babel, God has created something new in us. God does not leave us.

To confess Christ, to say that we follow and live *in* him, we must see how our bodies are being shaped by race and its attempts to order our bodies. We cannot seek a new word or believe that we have the eyes to see what faithfulness looks like. The Word enfleshed, the incarnation is God's redemption as presence, justice as a touch that transforms the systems that distort the beauty of my body. We need to see anew God's redemptive work in the world through the bodied Word, God becoming a human being who eats and breathes, who needs, feels the pangs of hunger and the gaping hole left in one's heart when your friend dies and his body lies in the cold dark behind a stone.

In this fragmented and disordered world, God holds us, even in our resistance. In the midst of our refusal, our deathly differentiations, God sought communion and presence with us. Abram and Sarai became a revelation of this God. In the face of death, God confuses the rhythms of identities. God's identity becomes entangled in a people, a people whose life with God is always bound to the life of the alien, the stranger. They are never the same as their neighbors, but their identities can never exclude the neighbor. They are never the same as God, but they can never be without God. Israel's identity is the melody of God's creative song. Just as humanity is bound to the land even as they are different from it, as we are like God even as we are different than God, God does not save us without being present with us. And God's presence confounds a world predicated on violent differentiation, racial or otherwise.

The incarnation is the chorus of God's redeeming work sung again and again in our story. The rhythms and patterns of Israel's life, their eating, their prayer, their walking, and their fetching water are steps in a journey with their creator. Jesus is born into the rhythms of these covenanted people, a people whose identity is bound to God, a land always present and always before them. The word is enfleshed out of *these* people, *this* ground.

Jesus's Jewishness is more than a historical curiosity. Race is a story that has something to do with our bodies and how we walk in this world, and with whom. This story of race is an ancient activity of identity. We might call it tribes or ethnicity or culture. But these claims animate and infuse our lives. To say Jesus is Jewish is to say God enters into these complicated stories. God enters into the complications of identity. I can trace my maternal lineage to the *Mayflower*, to a family called the Websters. My father's ancestors came to this land as slaves. My body is the holder of many stories. The Christian story is a story of bodies, of God's body, and ours—our stories comingled together.

Jesus saves us from the death of race. Part of what makes race so deadly is the ease with which we see it as natural, something inherent in us like the differences between cats and dogs or elephants and kangaroos. The idea that race is natural inserts itself as *the* story of my body. This fallen way of seeing and naming the world obscures our bodies, makes us more blind to who we are and who others are. And in our blindness we build towers to rise above the other rather than altars to kneel alongside; we kill fellow sojourners rather than discover new paths together, all equally being transformed along the way.

The birth of Jesus is the entrance of God into the world in a way that declares that our bodies matter. The child of a Jewish woman, Jesus is the fruit of a story, the continuation of a promise of God's presence, a people whose lives reveal God's life and name among us. In the face of the Babel that was the Roman Empire, God calls Mary and Joseph. In their language, in their prayer life, in their eating and working and cooking, God becomes a part of their household. Their neighbors and their friends, strangers on the road see God living with this family, and with us. God becomes our freedom seen in the day-to-day faithfulness of Mary and Joseph, descendants of the promise made to Abram and Sarai so long ago.

The practices and ways of life that sustain them are marks of the covenant that forms their Jewish identity. They are not a people without these marks, these practices. But these practices are not ends in themselves. Israel participates in God's life through ritual, witnessing to their participation with God in their obedience and faithfulness. By living into the law, the covenant, Israel becomes an icon. In their life they embody a truth beyond them, that God is present with all of us. The Old Testament is a witness to this unfolding drama of identity where Israel lives into (or out of) God's calling. In describing God's life with Israel, Scripture displays, again and again, God's decision for all of creation.

But even more, Israel reveals a God who has a name, a God who is this and not that, and a God who is transcendent and without limit, but is also particular. And in Israel's God, particularity abides with the world. Difference does not exclude people from promise, but offers points of relationship that make love possible. Love requires difference and freedom, distinct people (or communities, families, peoples) choosing one another and navigating what is not known, what is not like them, and perpetually bending toward the other in spite of what is not known, in trust that the other will receive us, bend their life into ours.

Jesus is the dwelling of this divine Word within the tensions and the joys of love, of perpetually choosing the other. The incarnation is the continuation of God's desire to be with us, for humanity to be free again. Jewish identity is an identity that rests entirely upon God's decision for the children of Abram and Sarai, God calling and God's abiding within. In Jesus's birth we see the fullness of this promise to be with us.

> Do not be afraid, Mary, for you have found favor with God. And now, you will conceive in your womb and bear a son, and you will name him Jesus. He will be great, and will be called the Son of the Most High, and the Lord God will give to him the throne of his ancestor David. . . . (Luke 1:31–32)

The angel's words to Mary, and her response, resonate with the rhythm of God's desire for humanity and our welcome of God's presence. Mary speaks of Jesus as a fulfillment of God's promises, an indication of God's abiding with and among. But not only does God associate God's self with a people, but God's redemptive presence is inextricably bound to the identity of this woman. Like Eve being molded from a sleeping Adam's rib, Jesus's body is pressed and pulled from Mary—the one made two, and flesh of my flesh, bone of my bone. Covenant becomes material in the world through the creation of a people, and again in the bodied presence of God. Presence enters into the world through a creative process that participates in the re-creation of our holy bodies.

As I become more and more immersed in Israel's creation and life, its wrestling with God in some moments or its profound faithfulness in others, I can't help but see the power of God's story to them and with them. They are bound to this promise and the God who uttered it. This faithfulness has made them a strange people who both always belong and are always strangers. But theirs is an identity of presence, their bodies moving toward God as they live into this covenant (and even when they don't).

The story of Israel is the story of flesh, the story of presence, the story of God's presence in the individual and in the social. God is present in the lives of women and in the lives of men. Redemption is a people being spoken into being from nothing. Redemption is the faithfulness of the alien woman who is subjected to a patriarchal system and yet becomes the kinsman-redeemer for a people. While religion has done so much to lubricate our pride and hubris, we also see in Israel's witness a constant refusal of God to be bound by the words with which we try to determine God and ourselves.

As God comes into our story through Mary, through Mary's people, God speaks a new word over the dust of our racialized bodies. The incarnation is water rising from the spring of Israel's life, singing to us that we need not fear our difference, that we need not erase it into a false sameness nor draw stark, violent lines of difference between men and women, Jew and Gentile, black and white, immigrant and citizen. The incarnation is God's word to us: I will save you by becoming like you, by being with you. We must tell our stories together. The incarnation is God's word to us, "This is my body, born for you."

A transparent Jesus cannot save me. Christian identity is about finding yourself encountered by a God who knit you together and now speaks to you through broken, imperfect people. It is about struggling to discern the ways God speaks sometimes more faithfully through those who are outside the church walls than within. Christian identity is about not knowing. But above all, Christian identity is about our bodies that navigate these realities every day, struggling within the mystery that is our own limbs and thoughts and desires, hungers and hurts.

The incarnation is a story about encounter and new birth. It is about the materiality of our salvation. But this encounter happens within a racial world. In a way, my encounter with God when I was sixteen feels like that uncertain call of Abram and Sarai. A voice comes from nowhere and my world is never the same. But God does not tell Abram or Sarai "I will be your God and you will be my people" (Exodus 6:7). God does not reveal God's name, YHWH to them. They have to walk in the wilderness, wait and hope for their promise to come into being, to be born.

I did not come to find the flesh of my encounter with God until three years later when I encountered my blackness in books, in the history of men and women who shared my skin and my straightish hair, who did not have the choice to check more than one box, or say "both." You were or you weren't. I saw pictures of men and women like me in chains, hung in trees, in books and art and song arguing their humanity with passion and beauty. And I read the history of how they had been refused, again and again. I saw the pictures of blood in the street and dogs with limbs in their jaws. I saw me twenty, forty, fifty, one hundred years ago and came to feel what had been encountering me for so long in my father, in classmates who asked me where I was from or why I was not with them. The story of my blackness had been a truth spoken over my life from my very beginnings.

I discovered a story that had been a part of me that I had felt, but that a Christianity supposedly without race could not account for. My white, Southern Baptist church and its deep piety could not help me make sense of my body and the work it did in the world. My body was still caught in hubris of Babel, being cut and measured to help others make sense of their lives. And if I am honest I participated in these measurements. It took the rejection of white girls (and their fathers) in middle school to help me realize who I wasn't, or at least that my body was more than what I thought it was. A transparent Jesus could not save me.

Blackness was not a language I could learn or a name I could claim for myself. Blackness was history that had always been submerged within. Reading W. E. B. Du Bois, I felt my eyes open to the water all around me. I was not floating above the danger. I was drowning. I could feel the weight of the ocean constricting my breathing and collapsing my chest. Until someone swam alongside me and showed me how to find the pockets of air, the spaces in this confined world where so many before me had found ways to survive, to resist the death beneath the water, to find lament mingled with hope.

In that encounter with the truth of my body and its story I came to realize how the death of race makes us choose, makes us narrate our story without the complicated overlaps and connective tissue. I was black. To say this meant I had to leave my mother, my home, in a way. I was born again into a story of a people who were perpetually marked for use, and yet spoke their humanity into being. In the cadence of their preaching, the sway of their songs, the blessed variety of their lives and laughs, I discovered a wholeness that did not require me to forsake my body, to pretend that those strange looks or ignorant comments did not exist. I discovered the beauty of my lips, of my no-longer-straight hair.

But I also discovered the struggle. I discovered that the rhythms and cadence of those sermons and songs were forged from perpetual resistance to the ways our bodies were spoken against, forgotten or feared. To be black would not simply be about what I would call myself. To be black meant to live into a rhythm of learning, speaking, teaching, working for the sake of these people, my people whose body I now knew I shared.

God answers the violence of Babel with the presence of a baby's cry. God takes up my body, our body. A cry that is answered in Aramaic by a poor Jewish girl in a dirty little town called Bethlehem. He takes on a name, a way of life, a language. And because of this I know that my body matters, that my salvation is not just a matter of my soul. God does not want my body to simply be stones for another man's tower. God does not want my life lived in scattered chaos. God wants our lives knit together, difference and sameness dancing with one another forever. God says to us, "I don't want to be God without you."[1]

Race is a word that we struggle within. It has formed and

1. Karl Barth, *Church Dogmatics* IV/1.

named us in ways that we can barely discern, and for some of us, see all too clearly each day. It is a word that is ever-present and enfleshed in our lives. But the story of Christianity is not simply the story of Jesus. Our faith in Jesus is also a faith in the God of these strange and word-to-flesh people, Israel. In their bodies and lives we can be sure that our faith is never simply about what we believe. Our faith is about the embodiment of a God whose life is love and relationship, justice and mercy, a presence that feeds and is fed, laughs and mourns, abides with and among. In the midst of our fallen world, a world so tragically marked by race and the deadly mispronunciation of what are bodies are for, Jesus is the enfleshing of God's life, the presence of God's life in our bodies, so that we might be free.

5

Jesus Walks

Gail and I were married in a little Lutheran church in the suburbs of Maryland. Before we entered we were separate people, Brian Bantum and Gail Song. We had no idea the significance of the words we were saying when we exchanged vows, a few sentences of promises we barely understood. But when we turned and faced the friends and family gathered there, we were different people. Our words had made us into something new. Gail's early mornings were now my early mornings. My disorganization was her disorganization. The words we spoke that afternoon knit us together.

Words are like that, seemingly innocuous inventions that, nonetheless, make two people one. But these words can also divide and subdivide, making people into less than a whole. Our fall, our cycle of violence and refusal of God and one another, is a testament to the power of our words, their power to create and de-create. Given this power, it seems fitting that God's intervention into our violence and suffering is a union of Word and flesh. From the very beginnings of our clever words that sought to justify ourselves and incriminate another, God seemed to continue to speak new words over us and into us, always making them flesh among us. This is Israel's story, redemption through the presence of God.

The story of race is the story of our bodies marked by death and dehumanization. Our fallen state is a distortion of the embodied word. Male is parsed from female, Jew from Greek, slave from free. But the relationship between our words and these bodies is never as simple as it seems. The binaries get interrupted by mixed children, women who can "do what men do," bodies deemed less than able, Greeks who seem more faithful Jews than some Jews themselves. The story of race is the modern attempt to organize these disruptions into an ordered language. The story of race is the organization of our bodies according to a word, a word born more in the sovereignty of the white body than any utterance of God. But just as God did not abandon us after our refusal, or leave Hagar alone after her abuse (Genesis 16:1–15), or Naomi in her mourning (Ruth 1:16–17), God comes near. God is near.

The incarnation is the continued song of God's Word to us. His conception and birth are promises of Word and flesh, marriage vows spoken over us that two will be made one. Jesus's life makes visible what it means to be human, to be made in the image of God. His life spoke against the tyranny and dehumanization of his time. But the life of the eternal Word also speaks against the sin of our time. His body is our redemption and because he lives his redemption stretches even into our present. Salvation is not about the state of our souls, as though we could be who we are without our bodies. The incarnation is a testament to the truth that our bodies matter, the ultimate refusal of the death of race.

Jesus's body *does work.* God's redemption is a bodily activity. Jesus's body, his presence, *does work.* When I assign grades to my students, those grades have meaning because of my identity as a teacher. If a student tries to give grades to her fellow students, those grades will not have the same meaning. The nature of my position gives my work a particular significance.

The incarnation is the presence of our beginnings, the author of creation. Jesus's body does work in our lives because of who he is. In the incarnation the Word is uttered as a body, a life that eats and speaks and laughs and mourns. But it was also a body that was subject to a violent empire. A male body in a society that diminished women's bodies. A body in a society that was fraught with ethnic divisions that had economic and social implications. His body was God's word to the individuals in those systems and a word to the systems themselves. Jesus's life was the restoration of God's image in us.

As Jesus walks in the world he lives into our human condition, into a culture, into an empire, into expectations of what it means to be a man, a Jew. His personhood transforms the patterns of relationship among us and within the institutions (family, nation, economy) that shape our lives. He journeys into the ways society refuses what God intends for us to be. As he walks he presses his perfection into our imperfections.

The structure of human redemption. When I first became a Christian and was introduced to the idea of sin I thought it was like a disease, something that got passed down from generation to generation and rotted our insides, made us something undesirable. This disease was the cause of everything bad in my life and the bad decisions I made. Jesus was the vaccine, the inoculation that made my insides clean. The incarnation was the birth of a person whose death would save my soul. The cross was the punishment, the necessary death that made my soul new. But what was the point of his life? Just to show me the decisions I should make once I was well? The longer I reflected on Jesus through the lens of Gail's life, of spirituals and Korean prayers, I could not separate his redeeming work from what Jesus did day in and day out—how he was living, who he was with, just how ordinary his life was in so many ways.

The incarnation is more than the birth of the person who will die. Jesus's life shows us just how central our bodies are to being made in the image of God, to being able to love God and love one another. Humanity's fall was not simply a condition, a sickness that is contracted from eating "bad" fruit. We are not in a perpetual state of punishment for breaking a rule. We live within a broken and contaminated society. Like a stagnant pool, the Fall dammed the streams of life and now incubates disease. Our world is still, murky water that shapes the way we live with one another. We cannot make it clean, and even the ways we try to survive inflict more death, making the water darker still. We seem to always manipulate the resources around us to establish ourselves, to protect ourselves, to find love for ourselves by stripping the freedom of others down to a husk. In his coming, Jesus enters our muddy pond and the distorted ways of life we have erected within it.

In the incarnation, the Word enters into this condition of brokenness and refusal. But even more than this, Jesus lives into our situation and into the rhythms of our refusal, pressing the perfection of his relationship, his freedom, and his unity of flesh and Spirit into our lives. His life and ministry walked through our experience, communicating peace to us, drawing us into communion with God's life.

When Jesus's clothes are stripped and he stands, naked, before the gaze of men, he stands with the child, the woman violently abused. He stands in a system where a woman's body becomes only an object of men's desire or control.

The power of the incarnation is felt in the people Jesus meets, each made in the *image of God*, to be loved and to love, for friendship and communion with God and with one another. In Jesus, God's life becomes present in synagogues, and markets, and in daily labor. His activities and experiences are enactments of our humanity and enactments of divine love. If Christ's obedience becomes our obedience, if Christ's birth is our birth, if Christ's death is our death, then it is not simply the individual that Jesus meets as he walks throughout Judea, he meets us all, he meets the systems that shape our lives together.

Jesus walks into the structures of gender, class, nation, and empire. He enters into the binaries our words have created to make sense of one another's bodies: male/female, Jew/Greek, slave/free . . . black/white? gay/straight? citizen/illegal? As he enters, he is the activity of God in these social systems, rejecting their dehumanizing work. God's redeeming work in the world is enfleshed, embodied, walking through towns occupied by military force, women and men subjected to religious, political, and economic power that does not see their humanity or their flourishing as their purpose. The perfection of God's life is pressed into our lives from the very beginning of his life, not only in Jesus's resurrection.

Jesus's interaction with the Samaritan woman at the well reveals the way Jesus presses into the life of the individual and the system that marginalizes the individual.

> Now he had to go through Samaria. So he came to a town in Samaria called Sychar, near the plot of ground Jacob had given

to his son Joseph. Jacob's well was there, and Jesus, tired as he was from the journey, sat down by the well. It was about noon.

When a Samaritan woman came to draw water, Jesus said to her, "Will you give me a drink?" (His disciples had gone into the town to buy food.)

The Samaritan woman said to him, "You are a Jew and I am a Samaritan woman. How can you ask me for a drink?" (For Jews do not associate with Samaritans.) (John 4:4–9)

In this story Jesus encounters a woman whose identity is marginalized on multiple fronts. She is a woman—an inherent deficiency in the cultural space of the first century. But in addition to this she is a woman who has been divorced four times and is now living with a man who is not her husband. Rather than fetching water in the cool of the morning, she was getting water by herself at midday, in the dangerous heat of the sun. She walks to the well each day as impure, unclean, an outsider. Who knows if the other women told her what they thought, or simply refused to speak with her when they met her in the morning?

The heat and her lack of fellowship were physical reminders of her place in her community. And even more than this she was a Samaritan, a people related to Jews, but who had been named as unclean because of their intermarriage with non-Jews. A "faithful" Jew of the first century was known to avoid the entire region, taking extra time and more dangerous routes to avoid the uncleanness of the Samaritan community.

This woman finds herself alone in the community because of the story that was told about her body. The brokenness of the Fall is embodied not only in individual decisions, but also in the geography of a community. She is without the resources of friendship and neighbors. Her community is cut off from the benefits of the Jewish community because of the way Israel imagined faithfulness as spiritual purity rather than an embodied life with the other. These stories become physical presences in the world that individuals must navigate and survive.

I wonder if she thought wholeness was something even possible for her. When Jesus asks her for water, engages her in conversation, he is transgressing a profound cultural/spiritual boundary. She reminds him: "I am a Samaritan and you are a Jew." But Jesus responds, "If you knew who asked you. . . ." He seems to say to her, "Your beginning, the healing of your grief, is present in this moment. She can't see it or even hear it completely, but it rings from Jesus's words and in her ears. The Samaritan woman is not merely interacting with a faithful Jew, but encountering the very presence of God.

God has come near to her. The very constructs of division are being unraveled and knit together again. First, the woman's painful life is brought to light: "It is true that you have no husband. . . ." In encountering Jesus she is confronted with the ways her life has been subject again and again to male power. When I was younger this story and Jesus's accounting of her previous husbands was a mark of her infidelity, a sign of her uncleanness. Her community has left her to survive on her own, a woman with multiple husbands, seeing her as contrary to what a woman should be. She was surely seen as promiscuous and unfaithful. But perhaps Jesus speaks these words not with judgment, but compassion in his eyes. Perhaps he sees the bruises on her neck and wrists and sees impossible choices a woman faces when subjected to violence in a patriarchal world. That so many find it easy to see her plight as of her own making is just another sign of our fallen social lenses. So Jesus offers her water, offers her

Spirit, offers her a fullness of life that comes from a deep and vital communion with God. Jesus says to her, "God sees you, God knows your name and the way this town has rendered you invisible." As with Hagar in the desert so long ago, God comes alongside her, but not as voice or command. God is present in a person who asks for water and whose voice stirs the woman's ears. She is known. She is needed. Jesus invites her to participate in the good news of God's transformation of the world.

Jesus's life and ministry carries this promise and possibility into the many various realities of human loss and longing. Bodily pain, social isolation, the loss of loved ones, desire for wealth and security, the idolatry of faith—Jesus comes into contact with the fundamental experiences of human life and touches them, communes with them, heals them. These moments are signs of the reality Christ is creating in the very air we breathe and the dirt beneath our feet. The healing of the blind and the restoration of the lame are foretastes of the deep truth of Christ's presence in the world. As he submerges more deeply into the realities of our experience, we receive new life from the eternal Word made flesh.

Even as Jesus enters into individual relationships and restores us, we cannot discount that he also walks as a man in a patriarchal society. He walks as a marginalized Jew in a colonized land and a society where Jews have also marginalized others. Jesus inhabits the individual experience of being human. But in assuming the fullness of our condition the eternal Word also comes to participate in the social structures we have built.

As Jesus interacts with the woman at the well, Jesus also enters into the social stigma of male-female interactions and Jewish-Samaritan interactions. In doing so, the eternal Word draws close to a woman. This small act is not merely an example to be followed, but re-creates a rhythm of relationship between men and women. In this communion Jesus calls a woman into communion with himself and through his transgression of the social boundaries disrupts the patriarchal system erected around us all. No longer can a man suggest a woman's place is behind him, no longer can I claim a woman's place is perpetually outside, because in Christ the eternal Word has brought the interactions of men and women into his identity and created a new reality. To perpetually divide men and women, to suggest a woman's place is below a man's, that a woman's voice cannot speak truth or insight, is to deny the new reality that Christ wrought in the world when he simply sat down with that woman at the well.

Jesus's interaction with the woman communicates a reorienting of ethnic and cultural divisions. Jesus's Jewish body is one that is irrevocably bound to a people. He is a rabbi, circumcised, and observes the law to its deepest truth. In his interactions with this Samaritan woman he draws the very beginnings of Jewish existence, the very calling of Abram and Sarai into contact with this Samaritan woman. He draws the fullness of her Samaritan life into communion with his Jewish body. Jesus invites her to participate in the fullness of God's life. The divisions that constitute Jew, Greek, Samaritan, become bent and reshaped into a new humanity where kinship with Jesus is kinship with those who are seemingly strangers or even enemies to us.

Gail and I left that little church as a new person. The words we spoke would now have to be respected in listening to one another, doing dishes when the other has had a long day, foregoing the promotion. We lived into those words with our lives. The word speaks to us in Jesus's life and love in the everyday.

Jesus has come for our bodies. When I was first saved I knew being a Christian had something to do with my body. I knew it meant what I shouldn't do with it. Don't drink. Don't lie or cheat. Definitely don't have sex before I was married. That was about it. And be kind, be nice. It was not until I began to see the ways my body participated in the larger stories of race and gender that I began to see Jesus's body had more to say about who I was with, who I was for. Race shaped my everyday. Living as a disciple would mean I would need to see my body and my world in new ways.

Jesus enters the very patterns of our lives and of the social structures that shape us. He was a citizen, a Jew, a son, a friend. He worked to sustain himself and his family. As he lives into these daily realities he also reshapes them. He bends the structures he lives within. He breathes something new into them that untangles the gnarled claims of hierarchy and power. As I read of the prophetic witness of so many black churches, the creative resistance of Korean immigrants and their children, I came to feel the weight of a life with Jesus. I began to read Jesus's life differently, feeling the surprise as he walked into defiled homes, feeling the tension of the self-righteous Jews as he knelt beside the lame and asked about their souls and their legs.

If we follow Jesus, we must follow him into the new patterns of embodied life that he enacted. His life refused the binaries of male and female, Jew and Greek, rich and poor. He lived into the systems that governed his society and continue to shape my story and the story of my body. In his life, words that divided and subdivided were refashioned to make wholeness possible. In his coming near to the Samaritan woman he offered her a freedom from the chains of her community's confined imagination. She left the well whole, empowered to confess the freedom that was possible for all in her community, even those who had rendered her alone and worthy to be beaten.

We cannot hope to overcome the death of race if we are unwilling to confront the systems of racism, sexism, homophobia, ableism, and classism. The totality of our bodily lives has been touched and restored in Jesus's coming. I am called to live into the fullness of his body.

The body of Jesus speaks of God's refusal to allow our illusions of independence and autonomy to remain. He brings the fullness of his freedom and offers it to us. The incarnation is our beginning as Christians. Our beginning is found in a God who chose a bodied life, a life that sought to learn what it meant to be human from a young Jewish woman. Our beginnings are born in a God who redeems us by walking into the tax collectors' homes, touching pus-filled sores of lepers on the streets. God redeems the bodily realities of our broken life because our sin is not a spiritual state. Our brokenness is about our eating, our homes, why we justify a black woman's death while we hold our own lives as inherently valuable and worthy of protection.

The incarnation is the redemption of our humanity—the restoration of the image of God in us. This image was not about status or good standing, but a reciprocal movement of love. We were created to love God. Our loving is made possible through a bodied life, a life that needs to feel and see and touch in order to know and be known, love and be loved. Our loving requires being confronted day by day, by one who is not us, whom we choose again and again to be with, who chooses again and again to be with us. Our loving requires care and thankfulness of the ground and its trees and plants and animals as gifts that sustain us, but of which we are also a part. Our lives require tending and care. We are just as fragile, just as subject to nature, as any other creature in this world.

The enfleshing of the Word is God's participation in our bodily condition. It is an expression of God's love that our bodily lives are blessed and good and what God intends for these creatures. In the incarnation God redeems our bodies. But this does not happen through the erasure of difference. Rather, the incarnation is the taking up of difference, declaring our histories as irrevocably tied up with one another. This redemption of our difference arrives as a strange voice heard by a young woman who is not afraid. What was so utterly different than us, hidden from us, is now seen and felt and heard. The incarnation says that God has come for our bodies.

Jesus came for your government and your guns, your human social systems. When Gail and I got married we were never our own people. I was a child raised in a home with divorced parents and with an extended family that got us through some tight places and was always there for us. It was a home of dysfunction and love, like so many. But that house formed certain ways of seeing the world, of navigating relationships, imagining what was possible for me. My wife was a person with her own story, the child of Korean immigrants, themselves trying to figure out what it means to be American and what that might cost. She was a musician, trained from a young age to have mastery over an instrument. This mastery cultivated strong discipline, extraordinary goals, and a belief that she could achieve anything. Our lives together were a joining of two people, but also two histories,

histories that lived in our habits, intuitions, frustrations, and joys. She had to navigate the history that was my way of living in the world, just as I had to navigate hers.

The story of America has been a persistent lie of individual courage and strength, ingenuity and faith. We remember the arrival, the conquest, but we do not remember the conquered, the used, the bodies whose labor built so much of this nation. The American story, especially, has been a story that resists its own failings and erases the contributions of the dispossessed. It is a story that seems, like Adam when confronted by God, to see itself as innocent. But in the incarnation Jesus refuses our desire for an individual salvation, to be seen apart from one another. Our stories are always intertwined with the lives of others in ways that we must continually discover.

When God comes to Mary and says, "You will be with child," God intensifies the abiding promise, "I will be your God and you will be my people." The incarnation is God's entrance into the uncertainty of our stories, to the dangerous ways competing stories so often end with death. The incarnation is the refusal of God to see our stories as different than God's story.

As we see Jesus move throughout Judea we see him refuse, again and again, any language that confines someone's possibilities to the accidents of how a culture interprets a particular set of bodily marks. The incarnation declares that our stories cannot be understood apart from one another. Difference is bound together.

Race is the inversion of the Word's incarnation. Race is the incarnation of human desire to subjugate difference, the difference of black bodies, of nonwhite bodies. I can't really say why race became the difference that was so violently seen.

Maybe it was just low-hanging fruit. But I suspect it has something to do with the subtlest disorientation of such a basic human function, sight. We see and our knowledge of the world, our experience of the world, is drawn in from the distinctions of shapes and color. The first human beings saw difference, male and female, humans from animals. They saw good and evil but did not know which was which, but tried to name them anyway. Seeing difference, they were afraid, ashamed. It was a tragic instinct that would grow malignant in such violent ways.

Race grew from the subjugation of women to men, the devaluing of women's difference and an inherent belief in the sovereignty of the male body. But from this root, modern notions of race formed systems that funneled dark bodies into fields or prisons, into unwanted corners of the city until they are wanted again, or ultimately dead by economic wastelands, subpar healthcare, urban food deserts, or police who cannot seem to dissociate black bodies from criminality and an inherent threat.[1] Even for those who find themselves fuller participants, we must negotiate constant, needling reminders of our difference, our hair, our eyes, our foreignness. In the so-called American dream, the dream always seems to be just that—a blurred moment barely in focus or always on the verge of being snatched by our waking.

But it is in these spaces that the bodied Word has already come near. Our Christian confession is tied to the racial realities of our contemporary moment. And these realities are not simply about dark bodies, but the many ways our white supremacist society perpetually silences any difference that

1. "Food deserts" refer to certain urban areas that have a high proportion of fast food restaurants while grocery stores (and access to fresher fruits and vegetables) are not as accessible.

does not sufficiently mimic the bodies of white men (or white women).

Jesus encounters us with God's *presence*, a presence in the ordinary—in work with saws and wood, fish and nets, hot stoves and water buckets, hungry bellies and cries of pain in the street as throngs pass by. As Jesus walks into those spaces he also walks into the systemic realities that shape those daily realities. Race is a system, a mode of de-creation that shapes our lives through the meanings assigned to our bodies. Some people can live most days without being reminded of their bodies—they occupy a space in the racial world where they can announce who they are—their quirks, idiosyncrasies, etc. But for some of us, we occupy the corners of this racial world where our bodies always go before us—where the language of bodies means one's intelligence must be proven or a woman's calling to ministry must be extraordinary to be acknowledged, if at all.

As we read of Jesus's life and ministry, he walks through a world where bodies have spoken before people could utter their names. Often the people whose lives he becomes present to remain nameless altogether, but nonetheless have been encountered by the eternal God. Their lives are part of the account—Samaritan woman, paralytic man, woman with the issue of blood. His everyday life, from his eating and sleeping to his grieving, centered on these people's lives. Jesus's life seemed to exhibit less concern about what you do with your body than who you are living among and who God desires to be *with*.

Jesus's incarnation, life, and ministry reverse the knots of autonomy sowed by Adam. Where Adam once said "this one you gave me," instantiating a nameless person in his midst, refusing her personhood in order to establish his own, objectifying this one who was his flesh and bone and blood—the incarnation is a word to us, "this one I give to you," and God dives into our womb and enters the world through our most intimate parts. I am your body. Your body is my identity. And so God redeems the first act of our transgression, speaking words of identity through the *embodiment* of the Word. "Let them be in me as I am in you" (John 17:20).

Race is the lie that I can be who I am, without you. Race is a system that makes some people's thriving contingent on other people's dehumanization. Christian discipleship is the confession that I am not me without you, and that our community is not whole while some are perpetually diminished. As we see Jesus move through our world, he reveals to us that God's justice is a touch that transforms, that makes us whole. His life of identification with us is a life that is lived for the transformation of bondage into freedom. Race is a de-creating word that signifies and separates; it renders some people always visible, always unique persons with names and stories, while other bodies are trapped within a story told about their bodies, making them utterly invisible or violently visible, unable to be anything other than their skin, eyes, and hair. But Jesus's presence in the lives of these men and women communicated something even more profound—a touch that transformed.

Jesus came to set us free. Jesus set the marginalized free to be seen, to carry their mats, to walk. But in his healings he is also transforming the material conditions of those who had been marginalized. He tells the lame man to pick up his mat and walk (John 5:1–18). As the man does so, he leaves that place not only in a new encounter with God, but now has the possibility to live in the world as not simply the lame man on the corner. He has been given means to live in the world, to tend, to work, to speak. Jesus's presence in his life, his touch, repositions this man's body in the world. He can now live into a new mode of freedom in the world to be seen and to speak of who he is. The condition is not inherently less than the *image of God*—but Jesus uses this moment to make this man visible in a way that he was not before. The man's healing was as much for the sake of those who passed by him over and over again; Jesus's recognition and transformation of that man's condition was a word for the society that had marginalized his body.

There are bodies in our society that have been pushed to unseen corners. There are people whose lives are marked more by death than by life. Our bodies were not meant to exist within the confines of others' inadequate words, words that entangle the lives and possibilities of others and thus articulate our own freedom, exonerating us from our sinfulness and our selfishness. Human communication—the intersections and encounters of different bodies—always bears the possibility that our words will not be enough. And so the opportunity comes for new words or old words with new meaning. Our bodily differences are the incubator of creative activity. Jesus's touch frees those whose bodies have been confined. Jesus's arrival opens the eyes of those who are trapped within a salvation that utters proper confessions while so easily casting bodies into tombs.

Early in our marriage my wife was a worship leader. After leading the congregation through songs that declared God's love and power, the hall was thick with the presence of God. This was normal to me and to many of us who had been ministered to by Gail. After the service a young woman approached her with tears in her eyes. "You are the first woman I have ever seen lead in a church." In this woman's twenty-five years of life, every woman she had known served God only by taking care of children, cooking, or ministering to other women. But hearing Gail, she said the voice matched her own. She heard herself in Gail's singing. She saw herself in Gail's presence leading the congregation and in that moment saw an affirmation of what she had felt called to her whole life. For years she had ideas for youth group, for Bible studies, and had sensed a call to a ministry that seemed forbidden to her. Not only this, but she saw them as something unnatural to her—something God did not intend and must be associated with sinful ambition or envy.

Year after year I have had students of color, the day before their graduation, tell me that I was the first African American teacher they have ever known. In seventeen years of school they have never once seen themselves in the person who guides a classroom, who holds authority or knowledge in a discipline. We turn on the television or go to the movies and rarely see ourselves. To say that sin is structural is not to simply say there are economic and political systems that oppress and privilege, although this is surely true. To say that sin is structural is to say that our nation perpetually reminds us that people of color and women, and black women especially, were not made for those spaces, that our presence is *unnatural*. Viola Davis, upon becoming the first African American woman to win an Emmy Award for best actress, expressed her experience in the words of Harriet Tubman:

> "In my mind, I see a line. And over that line, I see green fields and lovely flowers and beautiful white women with their arms stretched out to me, over that line. But I can't seem to get there no how. I can't seem to get over that line." That was Harriet Tubman in the 1800s. And let me tell you something: The only thing that separates women of color from anyone else

is opportunity. You cannot win an Emmy for roles that are simply not there.[2]

Davis's remarks are indicative of experiences of so many African Americans, Latinx, and Asian Americans in this country. We live in spaces that were not made for us. And this disjuncture is not a matter of talent. The structural realities of sin shape a world where our bodies are constantly read and interpreted, given meanings that adhere to us like a mist. Our personhood is obscured, even as we see the world that so often refuses to see us.

Structural sin is the obscuring of our bodies—whether the criminal justice system, inequity in education and pay, violence against women, homophobia, a patriarchal view of religious leadership—its root lies in making the dehumanization of others a seemingly natural idea. These various systems of oppression are built upon beliefs about what is natural for us or for others. Imagine any stereotype and it equates characteristics with a natural inherent tendency in a particular people. And these seemingly natural characteristics are differentiating—they have a negative and a positive pole.

These differentiations began with gendered dichotomies. Men are independent. Women are dependent. Men manipulate and work the land, killing creatures or creating tools. Women's work is natural work where children grow in their womb; the infants are fed from their breasts. Somehow these are not seen as signs of agency or skill or intelligence or strength. What is natural is dismissed or overlooked. Or, what is natural disqualifies someone from work in a world where an imagined independence is valued. From these

2. Michael Gold, "Viola Davis's Emmy Speech," New York Times, 20 Sept. 2015. Web. 22 Oct. 2015.

differentiations we see societies and cultures expect leadership from some and subservience from others, as if God made some to know and others to be known, to presume guilt in some and innocence in others. Over time, it is not the first or second or third husband fetching water in the middle of the day, but the Samaritan woman who has been ignored by all until a Jewish rabbi appears by her well.

The one who sits at the well in the heat of the day is the son of Mary and the son of God. He is the one who is the author of our existence and the one whose steps follow the ebbs and flows of our human conditions. Jesus is the water. He is redemption being pulled up and poured out for her. But this encounter is not about her alone. Jesus touches the very structure that rendered her body something lesser than his. He transgresses the boundary of Jew and less-than-Jew when he calls out to her. As he does, the lines of ethnicity (or race in our contemporary moment) are reconfigured, taken apart and put together in a new way.

This movement is true of Jesus's life and ministry. The structure of the state—an economy, taxes, conquest, colonization—is a desperate balancing act trying to maintain control over the bodies in its midst. Jesus's walking and preaching subvert these structures, knitting a new economy, a new meaning of our bodies, a new logic of difference, and a new kinship. Jesus knits us into a new structure of faith, hope, and love. In the incarnation—if we believe it to be truly human and divine—Jesus transforms people's lives, touching them individually as well as the structures, policies, and economies that gave birth to their marginalization.

Jesus's life and ministry create a new pattern of economic, social, and political life, fragmenting the violent differentiations of our world, if we have the eyes to see. In the very incarnation Jesus extinguishes the delusional structure of men as the bearers of God's image, of being the sole mediator of God's presence. Mary is not simply a womb, a vessel through which God arrives into this world. Mary is one who has read Scripture faithfully, her *Magnificat* recalling God's promises. Mary's obedience to the vocation of following and opening her life to God's presence leads her to mediate God's very life into the world. From this moment on, to deny that women can be priests and pastors, that they should be teachers and prophets, is to deny what God has done in Mary.

And Jesus's life was a perpetual unfolding of this new kingdom. His was a law of love, a presence that makes whole. His life was a word enfleshed for the freedom of those who are in bondage, oppressed by words of limitation (either those who speak or those who are spoken of). Jesus pressed against the religious claims that law was prior to a person's nourishment. He refused the assumption that the unseen of our communities are, somehow, not seen by God. He resisted a tradition that seemed to be more defined by its exclusions than by a love evidenced by its radical inclusions. He entered the spaces where oppression and subjugation were tolerated, even justified, because society believed these conditions were natural to those who suffered from its consequences, that God had ordained it. He entered these spaces and he touched, he healed, he called people by name and turned against the rationalizations and powers that found it so easy to justify another's silence or invisibility.

Race, ethnicity, gender, sexuality. These differences signify a story we have told about ourselves, or a story that has been told about us. The language of nature, of what is natural, has been used to determine what our bodies ought to be for and who they should or should not be with. Upholding

God's divine order, some might say. But in the incarnation, throughout his life and ministry, Jesus brought to our world a profoundly *unnatural* presence. Jesus's redemption is the *unnatural*, a structure of love where one body could be constituted by many people. He was a man without a "biological" father, his community an assortment of varied and not terribly competent disciples, many of them women whose roles were not merely sustaining the needs of the men. He had a habit of embracing defiled men and women while rebuking those who so easily called themselves clean. Jesus sees those the world has tried not to see. But even more, Jesus has rolled the earth in his hands and caked a holy mixture upon their blind eyes. The Word has come near so that we might see ourselves truthfully. Jesus has come to make us free.

Jesus takes up our death. As Jesus walks through this world, its structures begin to churn against him. In Jerusalem there were two structures colluding against him, the state and a religious institution built upon the certainty of exclusion. His death was the consequence of humanity's refusal to accept that their freedom needed to make others free as well. God came near and the powers hid behind fig trees and bushes of their own making.

Like God approaching Adam and Eve, Jesus confronts us. The trial of Jesus (Luke 23:1–25) is the reenactment of God's approach to Adam and Eve. "What has happened here?" "The one you gave me." "I wash my hands." "Let the people decide." "Crucify him." "It was not us. It was them." Just as God encounters Adam and Eve when they claim too much for themselves, humanity (the state and religion) are confronted by God. God's presence alone is judgment, an accusation and an invitation to seek communion. But like Adam and Eve, the Pharisees pass their guilt onto the state.

Pontius Pilate and the state pass their guilt onto the people. And the people choose the murderer. Jesus is not simply a lamb led to slaughter, but his death signifies the world's refusal of its own redemption for the sake of a shallow knowing. It is the state and its fear of the people's freedom that crucifies Jesus. It is a religion that has forgotten its unnatural beginnings, that fears the humanity Jesus confronts them with.

Jesus is crucified by the empire's fear of a people who might begin to taste their own freedom. Jesus is crucified by a practice of religion built upon the supremacy of certain bodies and the defilement of others. Jesus is crucified by a people who cannot believe that love can look like peace in the face of violence.

As Jesus is nailed to the cross, I wonder if Jesus is the placid figure we see on so many church walls. Is he a person who quietly allows himself to be pinned to the cross, taking punishment for transgressions of ideology? Or perhaps Jesus is on the cross as depicted by Brazilian sculptor Guido Rocha (Figure 1). Is Jesus the "Tortured Christ," the one who identifies with the pain and suffering and totalizing terror of sin manifest in society's structures? He is nailed to the cross for his opposition to terror and hate. He is nailed to the cross because his love is transgressive.

Tortured Christ by Brazilian sculptor Guido Rocha.

Upon that cross, his body pulls against the torment of society's refusal of God, his emaciated and suffering body struggles against the evil that moves through creation's veins. His screams of agony are mingled with a rage and anger that emanate from the very beginning of human history, that his creatures would kill and destroy and dehumanize one another so. This Jesus calls me to struggle in my everyday, to work every single muscle of my life against this tyranny. This Jesus calls me to a transgressive love and a perpetual call to confess, to make right, to speak truthfully.

And in the evening, before the stillness of the Sabbath falls, his body is laid in the tomb. The body of God, dead in the arms of those who loved him, is carried into the darkness. And even here he identifies with us; his body goes where our bodies have gone, where all bodies will go. He will experience the disintegration of our body and soul, of our yearning for wholeness. Because can we ever truly be whole without the bodies that make us who we are? And perhaps this is the most radical truth of God's bodily redemption. That even the structure of death itself will not escape God's redeeming presence. There is nothing God has not touched.

Jesus walked our humanity. As an ethnic man, a noncitizen, his life did not lead him to a heroic victory over the demonic empire. No, his life—taking up our condition—led to where it has led so many before him and so many after him. Jesus's body is broken, a refusal to maintain the illusion of our innocence, our vision of what our life ought to be. Race is a word that tries to name what our bodies are for. It is a word that describes whose body can be possessed or disregarded. As the powers in Jesus's midst begin to conspire against him, we begin to see the death of race unfurl its violence again. In the envy and pride of the Pharisees, the fear of the governor, or the delusion of the crowd, in all of these moments we see an incapacity to recognize or name the life that has come into their midst. They cling to the certainty that is before them, the robber, a crucifixion, a law only partially realized. Race is a way of seeing ourselves and others in confinement, through a singular lens that dulls our senses, allowing us to only see small slivers of ourselves and others and cutting out or refusing any parts of ourselves or others that seem to contradict those narrow definitions. The enfleshed Word, in his birth and life, walks into this death and its unimaginative and violent limitations. Before a crowd shouts "Crucify him!" Jesus encounters the death of race—a world of people who must kill an "other" to see themselves as whole.

Jesus's life says to us we are "bone of my bone and flesh of my flesh." Jesus's birth, life, and death was a wedding vow. Not unlike the words Gail and I spoke to each other in that little Lutheran church. We left that sanctuary different people. We could not have said how we were different or what our life together would be like. But who we were was intertwined with the other, and this relationship pulled on every string of our lives. We were different. Our families were different. Our way of life was different, even if we did not understand how yet. Jesus's life was a word of fidelity, of hope, of promise and love. His death was pressing that vow down into the deepest crevices of our life. He is not without us. We are not without God. And this means we cannot be without one another. His life must mean the death of race in us.

6

Jesus Makes Us Free to Become Like Mary

Someday I will die. My body will become dust. The natural processes of this world eat away our flesh until there is only bone. There will be nothing to distinguish me from the other bones that lie next to me on either side. You will not see my brown eyes or my freckled nose. You won't hear the way my voice changes just so slightly when I pray (or so say my children), or feel the excitement buzzing off my body when I'm about to pick up Gail from the airport after a few days apart. The spirit that animates my eyes, my smirk, remains. I do not know where my soul will abide while mourning and yearning for my body. I am not simply flesh and bone, nor spirit alone. They are both what make me who I am, fearfully and wonderfully made. In my death my body and soul will be rent apart and my flesh will be nothing more than an object in this material world, slowly decaying until there is nothing left but bone.

But death does not simply mean I no longer breathe or my heart does not beat. This physical death, the rending of my soul and body, is surely one aspect of our mortality. But death is also a life where society refuses the life God has breathed into us, a life where we are free to be with, to discover and be seen, to love and be loved. Race is a form of death because it renders certain bodies to nothing but bone. It eats away at the uniqueness and beauty of every individual and incorporates them into an ecosystem where such uniqueness is only possible for white bodies. Whether subtle comments of ignorance or derision, bypassed rental applications, or our ideas that remain always a side consideration, race eats away at some of our lives, moment by moment. Race is a system that classifies bodies in order to justify their economic and sexual exploitation, that renders dark bodies criminal, hypersexual, utterly invisible, and yet fearfully present. It paints the Asian body as perpetually foreign, the Latinx body "illegal."

But God answers this death. God answers, coming near to our decaying lives. This is clear as we read of Jesus's death and resurrection. Even as an infant, Jesus entered this death, as his mother and father were forced to flee the state's fearful wrath (Matthew 2:13). Even as an infant, Jesus was a refugee, seeking safety in foreign lands. His life and ministry conflicted with humanity's fallenness, manifested not simply in individual sinfulness, but in the sinfulness of a system that legitimated the pride and hubris that made the subjection of certain individuals tragically common.

Jesus's death is an affirmation of my life, of my body. Jesus is not Jesus without *that* body, that tone of voice, those eyes, that hair, that way of seeing the world, holding his mother's hand, laughing with his friends on a boat while waiting to haul fish up. But Jesus's death is not the only moment he identifies with me. His death pressed against the systems of death that abound in this world. In his death Jesus identifies completely and utterly with the fragmentation of our bodies and souls, his body killed not because of its crimes, but because of what it represented to the principalities and powers.

The incarnation is the embodiment of the eternal Word. It is God taking on the particularity of our life and longing. As the Word lay in the tomb, it identifies with the ways our bodies have been made into no-things by society, the ways they have been hidden away, killed, and refused. As Jesus lay in the tomb the Word lies next to the bodies cast overboard on the middle passage and next to the bodies lying lifeless in the middle of public squares. The Word ventures into the void where our spirits lie waiting for their fullness, where our souls are incomplete without these bodies knit for us before the beginning of time. But on the third day. . . . On the third day freedom comes near to us.

> But on the first day of the week, at early dawn, they came to the tomb, taking the spices that they had prepared. They found the stone rolled away from the tomb, but when they went in, they did not find the body. While they were perplexed about this, suddenly two men in dazzling clothes stood beside them. The women were terrified and bowed their faces to the ground, but the men said to them, "Why do you look for the living among the dead? He is not here, but has risen. Remember how he told you, while he was still in Galilee, that the Son of Man must be handed over to sinners, and be crucified, and on the third day rise again." Then they remembered his words, and returning from the tomb, they told all this to the eleven and to all the rest. Now it was Mary Magdalene, Joanna, Mary the mother of James, and the other women with them who told this to the apostles. But these words seemed to them an idle tale, and they did not believe them. But Peter got up and ran to the tomb; stooping and looking in, he saw the linen cloths by themselves; then he went home, amazed at what had happened. (Luke 24:1–14)

Luke's account of the resurrection of course does not indicate what happens in the moments between Good Friday and that blessed morning. We are left only with an empty tomb. Christ's submersion into the waters of humanity draws the realities, burdens, and refusals of humanity further and further into God's own life, touching the lives of those who are mired in society's refusals. Jesus takes our life into his own body, even unto death. There is no aspect of human life or longing that Christ has not touched or drawn into himself. This reception and giving extends even into a seemingly silent Saturday, as Jesus descends and enters into the very separation of body and soul, of flesh and spirit, with his body lying in a tomb, lifeless and alone.

This separation would not remain, though. The Father through the Spirit breathed upon Jesus's lifeless body and the enfleshed Word was made whole. Jesus was snatched from the very depths of death. Jesus's personhood was fully God and fully human, and he entered into the fullness of humanity. As he did so he took on our life. He not only took in the reality of a particular human person, but the fullness of the human condition, of every human being that is or was, because he was the one from whom every human being received its form and life. But in his resurrection, the finality of his death and our death was overcome. The resurrected body of Christ breathed his first breath and as he breathed, he breathed as us and on our behalf. Jesus had been slowly walking into our humanity, into the shape and contingency of our lives. The resurrection is a pouring out, a reversal. His first breaths in the tomb are our new breaths as new creatures. His first steps are the steps we will take out of our tombs, out of our graves, out of the deaths society has tried to hang around our necks. The stone is split and even the word "death" has new meaning in his body. His new life makes a new life for us.

As Mary runs from the tomb all she knows are the blessed words, "I have seen the Lord!" (John 20:18). In the initial moments of that blessed morning we only know that death was not the final word on Jesus's life and ministry. But in the subsequent days Jesus would begin to appear to the disciples in new and surprising ways. Whether hidden from them as one eating fish on the shore (John 21:1), or walking along with them (Luke 24:13–17), or appearing to them suddenly in their nascent community of followers (John 20:19), Jesus begins to display the extent of this new life.

The resurrected Christ is bodily resurrection. In restoration of his body we see the affirmation of our embodied lives, of the restoration of the very conception of human life as the Spirit breathes upon the clay and man and woman are born. The resurrection signals that the fullness of our lives is a life that is bound to the creaturely marks of our bodies, their limitations, their relationality. The resurrection is the sign of God's eternal decision to be with us, as us. In the incarnation the eternal Word sanctifies not only humanity in the abstract, but within the very real creaturely limitations of eating, walking, enjoying, and being with one another.

But in the resurrection we also see the beginning of a new humanity. Christ eats and walks and talks. He draws Thomas's hands into the wounds of his sides (John 20:24–29), drawing him into his humanity, which is healed but still bears the marks of its afflictions. This new humanity remains historical. That is, Jesus's resurrection does not lift him above his history, his mourning, or his trials. Instead, those who are buried with him are met in the waters of death and drawn out into communion with God. These marks do not signal his enslavement, but his victory. His wounded hands and side display the fullness of his journey and his lordship over death. But even more, his rising signals the overcoming of the powers and principalities that sought to entangle and consume him and all humanity.

Jesus's movement outside of the tomb signals the overcoming of death and the embrace of those who are death-bound. The resurrected body is a transfigured body that is both strange and recognizable. This Jesus with nail-pierced hands and sides has a face that seems to move in and out of recognition. His body is one that seems to come and go as it pleases. Jesus's body can be touched but it cannot be contained. His identity is revealed in some moments with the truth of his words and in other moments simply with his presence.

Jesus's resurrected body points us to the truth that death is not the final answer. It points us to the fact that in Christ even death has been touched by God and brought into the service of the King of Kings. But perhaps too, Jesus's resurrected body points to more than this. Jesus's body, his existence—the fullness of our humanity, the perfection of our freedom, relationship, and flesh/spirit—does not cease to communicate something to us, to press redemption into our bodily lives. Our new life is constituted by the presence of the Spirit; God's social life now identifies with and in us.

We are reborn as spirited bodies. When Jesus ascends into heaven he promises the disciples that God will send "another." "Another" of course refers to the Spirit. "Another" refers to the full revelation of the triune God in communion with and present in the bodies of these new creatures. But it also points to a Pentecostal filling, flesh and Spirit giving old words new meaning. For when Peter and the disciples received this gift of "another," what was "natural" burst open with something quite unnatural. The disciples' words were soaked with meaning that transcended their grammatical and utterable possibility. They were heard in new ways among kin and strangers alike. The Spirit came upon the disciples in such a way that their identities and their lives and their bodies witnessed something more beautiful and more transgressive and more political than they could have imagined. They had truly become "children of God." This kinship did not supersede their identities as Jews, as children who had been marked by God's words to Abram and Sarai so long ago. They continued to be Jewish, but this Jewishness was a presence of God in them that could not be held back by a curtain and could not be contained within walls.

The new birth revealed on Pentecost was that of children born perpetually entangled in the life of the Son, abiding in their very lives and words through the Spirit. Peter did not cease to be Peter, but he could not be whole without the recognition of God's presence that made him such. Just as Adam awakes to find one covenanted to him, made flesh of his flesh and bone of his bone, the disciples awake on the morning of Pentecost to discover that another has been knit into their lives. The promise that "God chooses not to be God without us" is no longer a promise of distant communion, but a promise of presence, a presence that we are still awakening to, but has nonetheless been made full and present in the resurrected Son.

Looking at the tomb from the vantage point of Pentecost and through the forty days between Jesus's resurrection and ascension, we can begin to see the tomb in a new light. Seen through the lives of the disciples and the new ways they inhabit the world, we see the tomb not simply as an indicator of death. The tomb has become a womb.

In the tomb the risen Jesus is the firstborn of humanity. Rising like a butterfly from a cocoon, he has drawn the fullness of our life into himself and pressed the fullness of his divine life into us. The resurrected Word is Jesus the Jew, the son of Mary, the one who has died, the one who has risen. And as he rises he presses into our flesh this new mode of human existence, this abundance of life where our bodies, our words, our lives might become pregnant with God's presence.

In the resurrection God's very identity is bound to humanity and humanity's identity is bound to God. We are a new people, sewn into God's life and through the Spirit are born anew. We are brought into our Father's womb in Christ's death and emerge new creatures whose lives are now displayed through the windows of faith, hope, and love, the deepest possibilities of freedom, relationship, union of flesh and Spirit. We are truly new creatures.

Jesus is the firstborn of this creation, rising from the tomb in a body that is both here and everywhere, his and ours. Jesus the embodied Word overcomes the structures that sought to render him nameless upon the cross. Rather than a sign of the state's power or the religious authorities, his risen body declares the fundamental reign of God and the blessedness of our bodied lives. He has come not just to save our souls, but the totality of our personhood. He desires that we be seen and that we be whole. He desires that we be fed and that we have the words to confess how the world is now different.

Be like Mary. If Jesus is the firstborn of this new creation, Mary is what our newborn bodies look like. Just as Adam was put to sleep and Eve was formed from his rib, Mary would wake with a new Adam knit from her. She conceived more than a child in that moment. God was enacting the transformation of our personhood. Mary's body is bound to God in the life and longing seen so beautifully in the Magnificat.

> My soul magnifies the Lord,
> and my spirit rejoices in God my Savior,
> for he has looked with favor on the lowliness of his servant.
> Surely, from now on all generations will call me blessed;
> for the Mighty One has done great things for me,
> and holy is his name.
> His mercy is for those who fear him
> from generation to generation.
> He has shown strength with his arm;
> he has scattered the proud in the thoughts of their hearts.
> He has brought down the powerful from their thrones,
> and lifted up the lowly;
> he has filled the hungry with good things,
> and sent the rich away empty.
> He has helped his servant Israel,
> in remembrance of his mercy,
> according to the promise he made to our ancestors,
> to Abraham and to his descendants forever. (Luke 1:46–55)

Mary mediated God's presence, displaying wisdom and discernment of God's unfolding story. She read the promises of God and could see when that Word was coming to fulfillment in her midst. But even more, as this word came to her in strange and troubling ways, she subjected herself to the ridicule, the scorn, the abandonment that such a following required.

She did not know that Joseph would still marry her. She did not know that her life would become a series of flights from city to city as the empire wanted first to count her head and then to kill her child. She was courageous in a way that most of us could not and cannot know. And through her courage and faithfulness she became a mediator of God's presence, a priestess whose body is the holy of holies, the innermost chamber of God's temple. To see her is to see the mother of God and our humanity. In Mary, God renews the possibility of our bodies. Mary is the first of these new priests, those who speak of God in their lives with courageous speech, bearing a radical presence, and following God into unknown places.

When Mary approaches the open tomb, flowers in hand, we see new birth not only in the empty tomb, the body that is not there. We see the birth of these new creatures in Mary's body and life. She is the one who first felt her creator's body enter this world, and now she bears witness to the absence that is the fullness of God's presence. In her life we see a glimmer of the freedom this new life begins to open up for us. Her life is the image of the *image of God* that the incarnation pressed back into humanity. In Mary we see three aspects of our redeemed humanity.

Mary is the first priest, a body bound to God. Whenever I see a woman or a man in a clergy collar I think of God and the church. I think of a life devoted to God and am reminded that there are people whose lives are set apart for the sake of this God who loves us. The uniqueness of the *image of God* in humanity is not simply about a shirt or an ornament. We are made of flesh and Spirit; our existence as human beings is permeated with the holy. Our bodies are white tabs on black shirt collars. Our bodies were intended to speak this deep truth, that God created the world to be with it and created us to enjoy that presence. Bodies (and the differences inherent in them) are signs that God's presence is with us, that a difference and likeness cohere within us. Mary's body was not simply a receptacle for God's redeeming work. Her body was the image of what all of our bodies could be and became through the Word enfleshed. We are a royal priesthood, embodied temples, and dwelling places of God's life.

Mary is confessor. As the angel approaches Mary with what will happen to her, she praises God, singing, "He has helped his servant Israel, in remembrance of his mercy, according to the promise he made to our ancestors, to Abraham and to his descendants forever" (Luke 1:54–55). Mary's song of praise is the confession that God has seen her, has named her out of all people who could have been named. God has seen her story and her life amidst the suffering of her people. Mary puts her individual life and her people's suffering in relationship to the promises of God in the history of Israel. Her song displays the interconnection between the person and the people, between the one and the many. Mary does not say, "Oh, I am nothing." She says, "All generations will call me blessed." She confesses what must be true in this moment—that if God has come to her, her life must have meaning. In a world where her body should mean very little, she understands that God's words to her subvert the story that had been told about her body.

Her song is not only a confession that resists the patriarchy of her society. She also expresses the wonder of God's redemption through her particular body. The entire history of God's relationship with the world, God's relationship with Israel, is being pressed into fruition through this one young woman. Drawing a line from her body to the promises of God to Abraham, Mary's life speaks. Mary preaches.

Mary is the first disciple, the first follower. The *image of God* is a bodied reality. This image is the grafting of dust and Spirit. It is the cohering of our words with the truth that we are creatures and persons with a history, all of which is tied to God's interaction with the world. But to say that the *image of God* is about our bodies is also to say that our lives must follow, must live into the truth of what our bodies are and what our words confess. Mary's life did not simply birth the bodied Word. She followed. This life was not fantastic but mundane, even in its perilous moments. Hers was a life lived along roads—to Egypt, to Bethlehem, to Jerusalem, to Golgotha. Hers was a life that walked with Jesus in the midst of the everyday—to the synagogue on Saturday, to a wedding in Cana, along the lake to eat fish. I can't imagine this is where she thought the roads would lead. But she followed, one step after another, walking to confess, her body speaking in every moment.

The image of women as first disciples is seen again in Mary Magdalene and Mary the mother of James and Salome, whose following led them to a tomb with their friend's body lying inside, their arms full of flowers and oils to mark the place they thought Jesus was laid to rest. As these steps lead them to a tomb that is empty, we see the fullness of our redeemed bodies in these Marys' lives. The resurrection is the overcoming of the structures of death, the overcoming of the fragmentation of our bodies and souls. In their faithfulness, their following led them to the tomb that morning. And there they were the first to witness God's redeeming work, that in the resurrection God has declared our bodies to be free from the dehumanizing realities of this world.

The resurrection is the promise of freedom, the promise that our bodies are precious and wonderful and unique. The resurrection is the unequivocal declaration that our bodies were not meant for death, to be chained by words and fenced by assumptions of what is not possible for us. The resurrection overcomes the death of race. But even more than this, the resurrection is also a judgment upon the gears of oppression that sought to destroy Jesus's body. His resurrection is not simply the overcoming of an abstract sin or the individuality of sin. The resurrection proclaims that the injustice of this world will have an end. God has a name. God is a body. God's body liberates and transforms our bodies.

The risen Jesus has a body that can no longer be bound within structures of what is possible. His birth, life, death, and resurrection mean that the differences we imagined for ourselves, and the differences that society has created among us, can no longer be the central determination of who we are. God takes up our story and our bodies so that we might be whole. But in order to see him we must have eyes to see and ears to hear. Like Mary's society, we live in a world where the logic of race has built a world where our bodies are perpetually working, where our lives are being determined and overdetermined with deadly consequences for the oppressed and the oppressors alike.

We must see our bodies truthfully. In the wake of the resurrection we must ask how our lives might become like Mary, how our bodies and lives should speak. What will we see when we begin to look at ourselves truthfully? In the midst of our racialized world, so many of us are asking, "What will we do?" while others say, "I don't understand, I don't see the problem." This country is not simply in a crisis of race, but a crisis of vision. We do not see ourselves truthfully. How might we see? The blind man at Bethsaida helps us to see our calling to be with God.

> They came to Bethsaida. Some people brought a blind man to him and begged him to touch him. He took the blind man by the hand and led him out of the village; and when he had put

saliva on his eyes and laid his hands on him, he asked him, "Can you see anything?" And the man looked up and said, "I can see people, but they look like trees, walking." Then Jesus laid his hands on his eyes again; and he looked intently and his sight was restored, and he saw everything clearly. Then he sent him away to his home, saying, "Do not even go into the village." (Mark 8:22–26)

As the disciples walk through the town, they pass a man that everyone knows has been blind from birth. He was born and has lived his entire life never having seen. The disciples asked, "Who sinned to make this man like this, his father or his grandfather?" And so the man, simply waiting for the sound and feel of coins in his cup or food in his hand suddenly hears the disciples talking. And in this conversation he hears a reference to him. It's not his name. No one speaks to him. He becomes the occasion for a theological conversation. Even the disciples do not really see this man. Jesus replies and answers the theological question, but while he does so he turns to the ground and spits. He begins to press the moisture into the clay, turning it over in his hands. Like God in the beginning of humanity's creation, breathing into dirt, making mud to create human beings, Jesus now bends down in the dirt beneath this man's life. Then he presses this mixture of God and earth into the man's eyes, and tells the man to go and wash himself.

In his gesture to the blind man, his touch, his presence speaks a simple truth. This man is not an occasion for theological speculation, for the disciples to show off and demonstrate their deep knowledge to Jesus or to one another. No, he turns his attention to the man himself and presses the mixture upon his face and eyes. The blind man feels the heat of Jesus's hands pushing into the clay as it cakes his eyes. Some of us walk in the world with constant reminders that we are not seen. We are invisible. God sees us. We are not simply an occasion for others to speculate about political or theological ideas. And as the man washes himself, he must go to the pool. He is called to participate in his own redemption.

Can you imagine what this moment must be like as he opens his eyes? His whole life, he has been attuned to life without sight. He has smelled his way through life, felt others nearby through subtle currents of air, picked out distances as sounds soft or loud. The world has looked one way in his mind and now as he opens his eyes, the world is new to him.

So this man comes back whole, without a barrier of darkness, and can know the world in a way that he did not before. But when he returns he does not see Jesus, the one who healed him. There are only Pharisees, and they don't praise God. They ask questions: "Is this appropriate? Were you really blind? Is this the Sabbath?" The man then says, "I could not see but now I can see. If this man was a sinner surely he would not have been able to heal." The Pharisees responded, "How dare you think you can teach us!" And they cast him from the synagogue.

He was cast out for seeing and speaking truthfully. And Jesus hears about this and returns to the man and to the people. "For judgment I have come into the world so that the blind will see and those who see will become blind" (John 9:39).

To move from blindness to sight is to confess our limitations, to no longer cling to the delusion that we know someone's burden better than they do. Beginning to see is the recognition that we cannot determine how another frames their burden or their offense—to refuse to say, "I want you to tell me your burden in a way that does not offend me." We do not like to be told that we have hurt another person, especially if we think we did not intend to hurt a person. The recurring protests throughout the United States have often been met with rejections of the tone and method of the demonstrations. If the conversation goes further, many white voices begin to assert their confusion because vindictiveness or racial hatred was not intended. But this resistance obscures the deeper formations of our bodies, our stories.

Newly married, Gail and I were just beginning to figure out our rhythms as a couple. Dishes. Grocery shopping. Cleaning. Everyday things. One day she came home and asked what we were going to have for dinner. I had been home all day working on a paper for class, while she had been working, in class, and attending rehearsals since early that morning. I said, "I don't know. You didn't go shopping yesterday." I know. At the end of the ensuing "conversation" about roles and maintaining our new home, Gail said to me, "Do you know all of the things I have to think about every week?" And she went on to tell me about how she thinks about the bills, who is going to pick up our son, how we will both be busy on a Tuesday evening two weeks from now and we should probably get a sitter now. And those were only the first few.

I had not seen any of those things. I would come home and play with my son, change his diaper and be proud of myself. The pressures of masculinity did not press me to consider the intimate needs of my son. Somehow I was formed to believe Gail was simply "better" at those things. What Gail was asking of me in that moment was to consider our household in a new way, to open my eyes to the reality of what our house was and instead see what must happen, to think about this place as though it is mine and is dependent on me. I needed to wake up and ask myself what has to happen to get groceries and pick up children. I had been living into a story about my body, a story that allowed me to believe that I could choose my attachments, that there were not things in my life that required change and transformation. I had to see in a new way.

I also had to see how my lack of sight was a type of bondage for my wife. Caught in a social story about what was natural to her body, I participated in her burden. A burden doesn't go away simply because some people don't see us. There are deformed stories pressing on us all of the time. To see rightly is to begin to live into the transformation that Christ's resurrection has knit into our bodies. I have to allow myself to be seen by God and allow myself to be seen truthfully. We must open our eyes to one another and see ourselves more faithfully, to bear the burden of this work and follow God's call along difficult roads.

The blind man of Bethsaida shows us that our blindness is not the final answer. Even in the things that are more natural to us, God can touch us and help us to see in new ways. But in order for this to happen we must recognize our own blindness. We cannot write it off because we do not feel it. God calls us to more than that. We must also walk to the pool. We must enact and live into, grasp and seek. Transformation does not come simply by hearing a new word. We will not come to sight without seeking, bringing holy water to our mud-caked eyes.

If we are to live into the truth of being a new creature, our lives have to risk telling the truth. At a meeting with five others who are all white, a white person needs to ask the question before I do, "Why does our company look like this?" She must risk being the race-obsessed white person. She will not be the friendly collegial person that everyone wants her to be when she speaks truth. People will question her loyalty, her "fit." But to see is to speak the truth, to say, "I can see now and I will not remain silent."

Christ makes us free by taking on the condition of our bodied lives. He lives our daily existence and lived the everyday dangers and worries of a subjected, first-century Jew. In doing so, he pressed God's presence into the broken stories that had come to shape his brothers' and sisters' lives. His presence brought sight, brought the freedom to see and to live into the fullness of being God's creatures. Christ does this not through the instantiation of sovereignty, but through a presence that confuses the storied distinctions of Jew and Gentile, male and female, slave and free (Galatians 3:28). Jesus comes into relationship with each of these particular bodies, identifies with them, and thus identifies them with one another.

For those whose lives have been dispossessed by disempowering and dehumanizing words, the promise of freedom in following Christ will look slightly different. For the slave, faith will mean living into the truth that her dreams matter and that her life is something worth fighting for. For the master, faith will mean subjecting himself to ridicule when he does not distinguish between his friend and his servant or when he must recognize that he cannot be whole apart from his slave's wholeness. It is a freedom that renders each body into a confounding presence in the world. Christ's freedom refuses death by saying that our freedom is bound to the life and thriving of our neighbor. To be the presence of Christ is to refuse the stories of death in our society and become communities of Christ, images of life, of bodies imbued with God and made to be for one another.

Race makes us blind to the ways we are not free. It

makes us blind to the ways we oppress, the ways we try to cling so closely to an ordered and certain life, that we are unwilling to acknowledge the beautiful disruptions that come when some protest that they are not fully seen, fully heard, or fully free. Race is a word that makes us blind to the belief that perhaps we should not want more, that our words and our bodies don't really matter. Race is a word that so often makes us blind to our own beauty and dignity and possibility. But perhaps most ingeniously, race is a word that works because it so often does not have to be spoken to keep working. And as long as it remains invisible we are not free.

Jesus's resurrection points me to the possibility of my humanity, humanity displayed in Mary's body, humanity already present within me, and you. But this is a freedom that is disruptive and dangerous, a freedom that people will kill to maintain. When people believe themselves to be sovereign, to be whole without difference, capable of determining who God is for themselves, like Cain they will kill. They will kill and justify the death with words like *law, reasonable, tradition.* They might not kill people (though some will). But they will kill policies; they will kill initiatives and funding. They will kill the disruptive reminders that they are not alone in this place and that we all will need to live together eventually.

If I am to walk in the life of Christ, if I am to follow Mary and honor my body, I must begin to see the ways race decays and tears away the flesh of my body, though each in a different way. If I am to be free I must speak and live and work for the freedom of Christ in others. I must bear the strange tongues of God's presence in my body, and follow its call, even into strange and dangerous places.

7

Race Must Die

"White People," I said. We were watching a news report about the most recent serial killer or mass shooter and all I could hear were the excuses that were made for this man, but not for the black men and women whose faces had been flashed across the screen a few seconds before. I was home for Christmas and had just completed my first African American history course, the early seeds of my transformation beginning to emerge. My mother looked at me with tears in her eyes and asked how I could say *that*. By *that* she probably meant, speaking race into the air. But she also meant, "How can you associate this man with me?" Maybe she was even asking if I saw her as something different than me. Pretending the cancer isn't there doesn't keep it from growing.

I had to explain to her how I was beginning to see myself, how I understood my history and my body. I was becoming a new person. I did not see that new person as someone who was no longer her son or a part of her story. I don't think she understood, really. She had sacrificed a lot to be with my dad. She had endured ridicule and discrimination.

As an overweight woman she knew judgmental looks and unwelcome commentary about her values and life. There was something in my father that allowed her a freedom she could not have completely in a white world. But she didn't venture fully into my father's black world. In her own way, a life with my father was a life that, perhaps, tried to live into an aspect of dark life. In the end, my father was the end of her journey.

Having seen the African American story for myself, having heard the cadence of hope and perseverance, I began to see the darkness of my body and its place within the story. I did not want to have to choose, but in a racial world there is no easy in-between where we do not have to feel tension, push and pull, and sometimes tearing. My mother needed to know my story so that she could discover her story. "White" was a word that needed to be spoken in our home.

This was not just a matter of race. I was a follower of Jesus. To follow Jesus I would also need to confess my blackness. The whole of my body would need to be knit into Christ's body. The stories that made up my life would need to touch. That meant my mother would need to confess her whiteness. Her body was not inherently sinful. Confessing is making known, baring something, allowing ourselves to walk from behind the bushes and see ourselves as we are.

To follow Jesus is to see my story, our individual stories, our national stories and how race is woven within every thread. This is not unlike what it means to bare our lives for Jesus. When I confess Christ I do not say only the things about myself that I am most proud of. If I follow Christ I must bare the ways my spending, my web browsing, my vocational aspirations do not conform to Jesus's life. As a nation we must confess the death, the labor, the subjugation that helped to create America. And I must open myself up to what I do not see, what I have refused to see. In our racial world we must also recognize the realities that have shaped us so thoroughly we often do not see them until they keep us from living into the freedom Christ is creating in our midst.

A tale of two followers. If I am to overcome the death of race I need to see what it means to follow, to see myself truthfully. This begins with seeing Jesus's life as a bodied life. He prayed, lived into the law, and heard the promises of God spoken in the synagogue. To follow Jesus was to recognize the possibility of life and healing, or old ways of being as unfaithful, and to look for new forms of faithfulness. Following meant new practices or reimagining old ways of obeying the law. The life of following is finding ourselves caught between questions of who others say I am, who I say I am, and who I say I am not. The incarnation of the Word is God saying who we are and asking us to speak with Christ. This word is a bodied word, a word that requires us to account for the patterns and rhythms of our daily lives. The presence of this poor rabbi is the arrival of a question, "Who will you be?" But this question also calls us to consider how our identities, even faithful identities, cannot escape being tethered to people, to how and with whom we eat, with the privilege to not worry about how much something costs, or without the assumption that when we walk into a new community we will be seen for who we say we are.

We see these questions unfolding throughout Scripture and especially in the New Testament. The encounter between Jesus and a rich young man highlights the way Jesus's presence revealed and pressed the identities of those who chose to follow him, and those who ultimately could not.

Then someone came to him and said, "Teacher, what good deed must I do to have eternal life?" And he said to him, "Why do you ask me about what is good? There is only one who is good. If you wish to enter into life, keep the commandments." He said to him, "Which ones?" And Jesus said, "You shall not murder; You shall not commit adultery; You shall not steal; You shall not bear false witness; Honor your father and mother; also, You shall love your neighbor as yourself." The young man said to him, "I have kept all these; what do I still lack?" Jesus said to him, "If you wish to be perfect, go, sell your possessions, and give the money to the poor, and you will have treasure in heaven; then come, follow me." When the young man heard this word, he went away grieving, for he had many possessions.

Then Jesus said to his disciples, "Truly I tell you, it will be hard for a rich person to enter the kingdom of heaven. Again I tell you, it is easier for a camel to go through the eye of a needle than for someone who is rich to enter the kingdom of God." When the disciples heard this, they were greatly astounded and said, "Then who can be saved?" But Jesus looked at them and said, "For mortals it is impossible, but for God all things are possible."

Then Peter said in reply, "Look, we have left everything and followed you. What then will we have?" Jesus said to them, "Truly I tell you, at the renewal of all things, when the Son of Man is seated on the throne of his glory, you who have followed me will also sit on twelve thrones, judging the twelve tribes of Israel. And everyone who has left houses or brothers or sisters or father or mother or children or fields, for my name's sake, will receive a hundredfold, and will inherit eternal life. But many who are first will be last, and the last will be first. (Matthew 19:16–30)

The rich young man was a Jew who was offering his sacrifices, trying to do everything he could to be faithful. And yet when Jesus walked through the town this young man could sense something was missing. Something deep within him called out and sought whatever Jesus had. He went to Jesus and asked, "What do I need?" Jesus's reply was not simply a call to selflessness. This man had an enormous amount of wealth. In his whole life he had not wanted for anything material. He lived a life with very few contingencies apart from his faith. He woke up every day free, so free that he felt he could approach Jesus and say to him, "I need eternal life."

So Jesus looked at him and said, "Go, sell all your things." He said this because when he looked at the young man, he saw that the coat of his life had insulated him from need, from needing any relationship whatsoever. "I want you to give that certainty to someone else and then you can follow," Jesus was saying to him. "It is not about what you do that will give you eternal life, it is about who you are going to be that will determine your entrance into the kingdom." And the man went away grieving. He grieved because he could not fathom his life without the sovereignty his possessions afforded him. He could not imagine being seen walking from town to town with those poor fishermen. He was paralyzed with fear so he walked away, not out of greed, but out of a fear of what he did not know, of a life marked continually by the unknown.

In the midst of this the disciples watched. Peter and the disciples must have been waiting for Jesus to put the rich man in his place. And after the man left, the disciples asked him "who can be saved?" seeking to be assured of their sacrifice. As Peter and the disciples watched the conversation unfold, and the young man's eventual decision, I can imagine Peter's reaction. Peter had dropped everything, had left it all and followed without question. Peter's vocation was dependent upon the sea. If he didn't catch fish that day, he and his family would not eat. But even if he made a small catch, he must take a required amount to the tax collector. Maybe this time the tax collector asked for a little more. "Twenty percent today. If you don't, then you're going to lose your boat." Peter had no choice in the matter. His life was nothing but contingency, defined by dependence—on the sea, on his community, on his fellow Jews. When Jesus called him Peter heard from a place of dependence, a place where the entirety of his life was need. Confronted with a man pulling nets full of fish from a previously empty lake, Peter did not have to be told of his need, only shown that Jesus had supply.

But after following Jesus, Peter also began to discover the deepest truth of what Jesus offers to him and the world. In walking with Jesus, Peter received a standing, a coat of hope and certainty in the world. He was with the great teacher. But one of the first places Jesus went after calling Peter was to the tax collector's house.

What do you mean, we are going into that man's house? Do you know what he does to our community? Do you know how he has forgotten his people? Do you know how he has defiled the law? He has given up everything it means to be a Jew. Do you know we all hate that man? And you want us to eat with him? As Jesus entered that house he called Peter to be reborn. Like the rich young man, Jesus called him to give up his coat, the coat of respectability that he had just received, the coat of reputation, and the coat of maintaining his righteousness by being so sure of the tax collector's lowliness. Jesus said to Peter, I have come near to you so that you might come near to him. I have put a coat of blessing on you, but now I want you to give it away. I want you to clothe that exiled Jew with standing in our community. That is the moment of the rich young man, when Jesus looks at Peter and says to him, "This is what you are about; I want you to sell what is most fundamental to who you are for the sake of a life with me."

Jesus is God's Word to us saying, "I want to be with you." But this Word also calls us to see the ways our lives are tied to one another. Peter's identity had been navigated by imagining himself as someone very different than the tax collector. The rich young man was confronted by the fact that his material life was truly the center of his identity, even as he believed himself a deeply faithful Jew. The Word that had given birth to Israel was calling these very different Jewish men to reconsider what being Jewish looked like. Jesus was calling them to see the new people with whom they must identify if they were going to be faithful to what God has called them. Christian discipleship is being caught in a radical and dynamic identity that confronts us with who we say we are and who we say we are not, confusing and confounding both.

Jesus also knits people together—calls us to see ourselves as bearing one another's burdens, our identities coiled together. Christian discipleship is about an identity that is dynamic and present. We follow a God whose existence became radically entangled in human existence. We follow a God who has always subjected God's self to the limitation, folly, and violence of our inept and limited descriptions. But we also follow a God who *identifies* with us and for us. In Christ we see God say to us, "I want to be with you. I want to be like you and I want you to be like me." Jesus's prayer in Gethsemane, "That they will be in me as I am in you," is not a status, a frozen moment (John 17:20). These words indicate Christian identity to be a process of speaking with God, of living with one another, and discovering a freedom in recognizing the gift of difference in our midst. This can only be done in and through our bodied lives, living with one another in the mystery we are confronted with every day when we look at the lives of those who are near to us.

True confession is the activism of our bodies. In Christ, our story and God's story converge. He enters into the disease of our differentiations and refusals. Male and female, Jew and Gentile, slave and master, confession of his life is not a set of beliefs that we speak. Christian confession is an orientation of our bodies toward the love of God, toward God's body, Jesus the Word enfleshed, and the Word reflected in our neighbor.

Jesus brings us again to the beginning. He confronts us with a question, a question not unlike the question asked of Adam and Eve, "What have you done?" But the question is more than this. The question is about our identity: "Who are you?" Eve and Adam's eyes opened; they could not see in the brightness of the world, in the fullness of its glory and presence with God. They could not speak of what they saw. So they only spoke of what they did not see, what was unlike them, seeking to maintain their place in God's life.

"Who are you Adam?"

"I am not the one you gave me."

"Who are you Eve?"

"I am not the ground you gave us."

More than a confession of their violations, God seems to want them to confess that they are bound to one another, and bound to God. The illusion of their independence seemingly hardening, God drains the fluid of their Edenic life, allowing them to feel the friction of bone on bone and flesh with flesh. They will feel the tearing of muscle when it works too hard for too long. They will feel the energy spent to usher new life into the world. They will not be without one another, husband and wife, one with another. The land will kick and scream under their toil, flood and drought will remind them that they hunger and thirst. Person with person will struggle in the gaps of what they do not and cannot know. Their relationship became obedience rather than love, necessity rather than gift.

God's presence through the incarnate Word reveals the shape and pattern of our refusal to be with God. Jesus's life makes known the ubiquitous and varied ways our refusals have accumulated into systemic and social realities. These social refusals are embedded in the implicit and explicit acts that suggest that some were not meant to be free, that we are not beautiful, that our bodies are terror or seduction or lack of knowledge. And on the other side of these refusals are dangerous assumptions of one's independence, the presumption that one community's safety requires another community's over-policing or even bombing. On this side of white supremacy is the assumption that those in power are not bound to the disempowered, and perhaps most pernicious of all—that those who enjoy the privilege of white supremacy's racial logic bear no guilt, no responsibility.

Through Christ's life, God's story pressed into our lives, we participate in the new patterns of relationship that have become incarnate in Christ's person and work. Jesus's presence, his unrelenting love, uncovers the ways I qualify my confession. He comes and looks us in the eye and asks us to confess "I am seen and I am beautiful," or "I have been lost," or "I have been lying to myself." My confession never seems to end at the condition of my soul. I am asked to go back into the town that shunned me, or return to the village that passed by me day after day. I am asked to acknowledge that there are areas of my life that I do not want Jesus to touch and transform. In a world teeming with the cancer of the Fall, I am invited into a life of freedom, of wholeness in Christ's body. I confess this freedom with my life. When we follow the body of Jesus, our confession becomes a type of activism—naming the various ways white supremacy shapes our lives. Through this naming we begin to live a new story.

Following Jesus is a call to risk acknowledging that my security and certainty are due not simply to my hard work, but to a legacy of exploitation that siphons wealth to smaller and smaller percentages of the population. It is to resist the possibility that our lives really are contingent, subject to evil in a way that seems too big, too overwhelming to comprehend. It is to risk seeing the contingency and limitation of our bodies and just how insignificant our daily lives might be without the falsehoods of nation and America and freedom to puff us up each day. Adam and Eve's freedom was a simple freedom—to work, to be with God, and to be with one another. To wake up each day with one who would love you and try to be for you, and to abide in a world that was God's but given to us to live within. The ideas of freedom that insist I can be without you or that I am entitled to more safety than you, that there is no risk, is a lie that tries to give meaning to my daily life, a lie that is impossible to uphold or guarantee without death.

Living into Christ's freedom is not a call to colorblindness. Jesus's presence reveals the powerful truth of our faith—that our bodies matter, that our bodies do work in the world and testify and confess to something beyond ourselves. But our bodies cannot speak if we continue to hide when God comes walking through the garden. We are sinners and saints, but our varied bodies do different work in the world. Living into Christ's freedom is beginning to see the complications of our interconnections, the complicated ways our bodies are subjugated to this racial story, even as we subject others to the stories we have told ourselves. It is a call to participate in victory over death's consequences. Christ's life is a call to see our lives tied up together as God's life is tied to ours.

In many ways, this call is not even about reconciliation, or at least a notion of reconciliation that has seemingly settled what reconciliation looks like before all of the parties have gathered around the table. Living into Christ's freedom is a life of risk for all of us, a risk that God subjects God's self to in God's desire for us to rediscover the freedom to love that was knit into our bodies in the beginning. It is a risk God took in the incarnation; entering into the world with the possibility that we would refuse, even kill this Word to us, that we would choose another. Too often, the language of reconciliation presupposes a relationship, that we somehow know what the end of this process ought to look like, that in the end, I *have* to sit at the table of fellowship. This is not freedom, but another form of coercion. Too many reconciliation conversations funded by white churches do not risk the possibility that dark bodies do not want to be with them, that what nonwhite Christians really want is a life where their wholeness is presupposed.

The freedom embodied in the incarnation is a radical love, the insistence of God on justice and an invitation to a life of love. This is God's freedom. There is not freedom without bodies oriented toward one another for the sake of one another's wholeness. God endows us with a freedom to love and to be with. Even the incarnation, the most powerful sign of God's reconciliation, is not coercion but an invitation. God does not demand that we be with, but sets us free to love and be whole. True reconciliation is the fruit of two people who are free, loving and choosing one another, always with the real possibility that they could choose another, and yet desiring the one before them. Notions of reconciliation driven by white evangelicals, too often, want the end, but not without dictating the means—in a way, they want to set the conditions of their freedom, and of mine.

My body must create freedom for others. If we truly want reconciliation we must desire the conditions of freedom that allow a person to truly choose to be with us, and respect them if their wholeness can only be imagined apart from us. This difficult truth means that I must continually wrestle with the patterns of unfaithfulness in my life. I must continually work to see how I am working toward cultivating a spirit of freedom and wholeness in my small spheres of influence. But I must also be willing to see where I fail, where I am even incapable. As a lighter-skinned, tall American man, my life is privilege and subjugation. I must struggle to image the beauty of my face, the authority of my experience, the truthfulness of the God I see in the world every day. But my words are received more easily than my wife's words, especially in the church. People will nod in agreement to a word that is met with questions and clarifications when suggested by my wife. My body will not be a sign of freedom for the women in my class. The presence of my body may not signal the possibility of their vocational call to teaching in the same way a female body will. So in my space I must work toward a faculty that is diverse and displays varied images of academic life. Freedom means I cannot seek to reproduce my life in others.

Christian confession is living against the namelessness that empire perpetuates. Confession is to situate our identities alongside the lives of those who complicate our coherent selves. Christian confession is about the presentation of our bodies to God and to one another, slipping out from behind the bushes, dropping our fig leaves so that our difference can be seen. So that we can be disturbed by the difference that these various bodies, lives, histories confront us with.

We experience the world in different ways. We are in bondage to the lies of this world in various ways. To acknowledge our condition truthfully is to *see* our condition truthfully. The ways our bodies are mysteries to us even as we inflict certainty in others. The Christian life is confession of Christ as if our bodies mattered. This confession is to live always in between. We exist between birth and death, always trying to understand the histories and the lives that intertwined to usher us into this place at this time. We look behind us even as we walk slowly to the cessation of our bodily life, trying to make meaning out of our present.

We exist between creation and fall—seeking joy, relationship, wholeness, peace with the one who brought us into being and walks with us still, life with those who are given to us, who help us to taste and see life and ourselves most truly. We live in the fall of this gift, in its corruption, as every good thing that marks our life carries with it also the possibility of death: the death of another, the death of ourselves, the death of our dreams and our hope and our faith. We take what is most unique and we utterly destroy the world, all the while believing that destruction is a mark of our likeness to God. We all do this in little ways and in large ways. The dark man laments his bondage while he beats the dark women in his midst. The white woman cries out against her marginalization and objectification while she silences the dark woman who asks why her body is not present at the table. The country that lauds its own values of freedom imprisons innocent men and women for years for the sake of national security.

While we are all bound up in the fallen world together, we occupy different spaces and endure different pressures. We are knotted up together, but some of us are threads that are dangling while others are strands buried deep inside the tangle, and with every turn or yank the weight of the whole presses into our bodies without mercy or thought.

Race is the gravity of our present fallen condition. Its power draws back any body that tries to find freedom away from the ground. There is no escaping it. But race is not a description. It is not a classification. Black, white, Latinx, Asian American—these are the children of race, but race is an idolatrous tool, a pseudo god invoked to re-create the world in its own image. Race is not a description but a way of being—its henchman is whiteness and its chariot is the church.

If we are to live, race must die. Race is the present strain of humanity's refusal of our bodied lives. Race is the incarnation of a desire to live untethered from one another, from the ground. And if one cannot imagine living with others or as a creature with other creatures, how can they say they want to live or to know God? They do not want to be with God. They want a life independent from another. They want the independence of a god, a god that does not exist.

The truth of our bodied lives, of the story of our beginnings in the Garden of Eden, is that we cannot choose who is with us. We cannot choose the differences that will give us life or the differences that we need. The difference inherent in our bodily lives, in race, gender, sexuality, is the constant reminder that God does not create us to be alone. But the community of God is only possible in the embrace of the one who is not like us.

The freedom God endows us with, the beauty of our faces, our hair, our mouths, are small signals of a miraculous truth: we are created to be free with God and with one another. We live in a world where the possibilities of a people, whether their safety or their prosperity, are contingent on the suffering of another. We live in a world where there is a rampant lie of sovereignty; whether of individuals or nations, without seeing how such claims seem to constantly reserve freedom for some, while legitimating the violence, incarceration, and exploitation of others. This reality makes our society no better than the racist societies of antebellum America. In fact, it makes us worse because this society wants to enjoy the benefits without taking responsibility for what it seems to say with every overpriced organic orange it sells—dark lives do not matter.

If we are to live, race must die. But I do not mean an antiquated description of skin or hair. To say that race must die is to say we must refuse the lie that we can exist freely while others struggle to be seen as human, with possibilities and gifts and beauty. I do not mean we cease to claim names of black or white or Korean. For my children these are all aspects of who they are, their story. To say that race must die is to refuse the lie that my life with God can be whole while other people's futures are foreclosed. To say that race must die is to actualize your gifts, your vocation, your voice, and your body for the freedom of those in your job, your community, and your school and to work fervently to ensure that their lives might be imbued with hope.

To say that race must die is to say my mother's marrying a black man was not enough, that my having a black father does not give me a pass to do the hard work of discovering the story of my body and the work it does in the world. My mother needed to know the story she was binding herself to. When I married a Korean American I was knit into the complicated story of Asian American life, its in-betweenness and its beautiful community. But I also saw how so many of their lives were caught in the death of race, how difficult it is for some to see black men or women as their potential sons or daughters. We are all knotted in this together. For race to die I must become a follower. I must see the risk Jesus's body poses for my life.

8

There Is Life in the Tomb

When Jesus sailed across the sea to the Gerasenes he walked into a story. Who knows how the story began? But it ended with a man chained in the tombs while the rest of the town went along with their lives.

> They came to the other side of the sea, to the country of the Gerasenes. And when he had stepped out of the boat, immediately a man out of the tombs with an unclean spirit met him. He lived among the tombs; and no one could restrain him any more, even with a chain; for he had often been restrained with shackles and chains, but the chains he wrenched apart, and the shackles he broke in pieces; and no one had the strength to subdue him. Night and day among the tombs and on the mountains he was always howling and bruising himself with stones. (Mark 5:1–5)

This was a town bound by the death of race, certainly not the racism of our colonial world, but race as a logic that legitimated the binding of one man to create a sense of normalcy for the rest.

But it was not the man's condition that shackled him to a tree in the tombs, that hid him away from the everyday lives of the people in that town. Death permeated that city,

143

those people's lives, in rationales that justified this poor soul's double bondage. This man was chained, his body knotted to the dead, by invisible spirits/words that distorted the possibilities and perceptions of his life, rendering him strange to his own people.

When he was quiet or away from the town the people had a sense of normalcy. But when he would break his chains and come into town wailing and screaming and hitting himself, their everyday was broken; they were reminded of the "inhuman" in their midst. They could see their humanity more clearly, tell themselves that their life was faithful because they could care for themselves, they could sustain themselves. Their life was normal when he was absent (or at least invisible).

And yet, this man broke from his chains. Seeing life itself walk down the path, his humanity sought freedom from the words that chained him. From the tombs he ran, his body still reeking of death, his ankles raw from the marks that his town had burned into his body.

As the town came to see what happened, they did not see new life. They did not see their bodies and souls restored. Instead they lamented the loss of their swine, their economic certainty, their comfort. The presence of Jesus in this town revealed not only the humanity of the exiled and rejected, but also how the tombs were not confined to the edge of town. Gergesa was a town circling around death—its life sustained only by the illusion of the citizens' estimation of their own humanity, the purity and normalcy of their identity made possible by the sending away of this man into a wilderness, the words of "other" marking his body to make the people clean.

As the townspeople mourned their animals, their own

possessions, *their* inhumanity came into focus. They resisted the presence of the holy one. They begged Jesus to leave them so that they might rest in their delusion once more. I can only imagine the once chained man, now standing before the people of the town and Jesus. He looks from Jesus to the people who tied ropes around his feet and chained his wrists. Now, he calls them by name, wanting to be rejoiced, to be received again as one whose life mattered. But they did not see him. They swam in a fallen freedom, a freedom built upon their capacity to choose, to buy and sell, to pursue happiness. Freedoms made possible through the enslavement of another, rendering one's words, face, and way of being so ab-normal that they are driven mad. Mourning the pigs rather than the life in their midst.

Our bodies, material as they are, are never disconnected from others. My life is a mysterious intermingling of my mother and father, teachers, friends, antagonists, and my various good, bad, and indifferent responses to their lives and actions. My life is the consequence of my mother's courage even if that courage was uncertain and uneven. She was determined to insulate me from the violence of her youth. Her life made a freedom possible for me. Because of her and so many others in my life, I have to hope. Despite the ubiquity of this deathly thing called race, people continue to speak their humanity, to fight for their fullness through marches, the occupying of presidential offices, and the quiet but persistent bending of institutions.

The incarnation is the invitation to live into a new story. The incarnation is the promise that our bodies and our words matter, that in the union of flesh and Spirit there is a creative power to love, and that truth is unrelenting because it, too, is part of God's life. To be a disciple is to embrace the beauty of our bodies and the realities of our stories. To be a disciple is to dwell in Jesus's overcoming of death. From the time I checked the box as a six-year-old, my body has been marked by race. There was a time when I would not have believed such a claim. Even when I did not think I was negotiating realities of race, I was aware of looks, of glances. As I heard the same story of suspicion or dismissal from so many students, fellow faculty, and people in my congregation, I saw them trying desperately to navigate the subtle and not-so-subtle pressures of race. To be a disciple is to embody the freedom Christ embodies in the world and has knit into our bodies in the incarnation.

In the beginning of this book I suggested that race is a story. It is a story written onto our bodies and the patterns of our society. The story takes time to form, beginning with questions. "Who are those people? Why are they so different than us? How do we begin to make sense of those differences?" Like earth slowly compressed over time, the various stories that come from these questions harden, becoming stones from which walls and towers are built, the structure of a city and a people. After some time we forget that the walls were questions first, that the answers we came up with were based on questions asked by people with limited vision. Eventually, the stories of people on the outside of the walls or the people hauling the stones for our roads, harvesting our crops for little or no pay—the stories of their (and our) beginnings are lost to nature, to explanations that are no longer connected to history, but are simply ways to justify one person's wealth and another person's poverty, the annexation of another people's land, a woman's silence in church, or the justification of barring refugees fleeing from violence in their own lands.

But when we return to the stories of Jesus's life, we see there is no story that Christ has not taken into his life. His life with us declares to us that we are beautiful and powerful and invites us to speak and live out our dignity. We live into Christ when our lives press against the de-creations of our contemporary world, when our lives work to affirm the fullness of all people.

Jesus allows us to see life in the tombs. Race is a structure of death. The lies concerning our bodies, their uses and their limitations, are knit together into an all-encompassing system, an ever-present gravity pulling our bodies down into a disordered order. In this system we are subjected to lives in tombs, to a nameless dismemberment where our bodies are associated with death, with a humanity that is always connected to an elusive whiteness, an impossible transcendent specter of perfection that can never be fully grasped, only imitated.

In the incarnation we are confronted with a radical freedom. The Word enfleshed is a body that is *for* us, so profoundly for us that we recognize our lives as meant for something more than death, that our lives are not intended for the decomposing corners of society. Our bodies were not made for chains made from social hubris. We were made to be seen and called by name, to share and tend with, to make one another's humanity clearer and fuller each day.

The Word enfleshed enters our lives, calling us from the tomb in which society has sought to confine us: tombs of race, bars of criminality, tethers of incompetence, and ropes of "not enough." As Jesus walked into town past the tombs, the man glimpsed life. When we see and feel the possibility of our freedom we break free, cry out for wholeness, defying the death that society ascribes to us. And God's body has heard our cry, allowing us to see ourselves as beautiful, as free, with power and possibility.

In the incarnation we are encountered by a God who desires us to be free, to break free from the yoke of demonic social constructs that constrain our minds and the systemic chains that limit our bodies. We are meant to be free; free to enjoy the ground, to walk and work with one another. Freedom is the unity of our bodies, souls, and minds to create and love, to know and be known. From his place in the tombs, that man believed the impossible: that he did not belong among the dead.

We are all struggling against the way race presses our bodies and the possibilities of what our bodies are. Jesus confronts our assumptions about what our bodies are for. He comes beside those whose bodies have come to mean everything about them, rendering them unseen. But he also confronts the identities of power, the identities that hide behind a normalcy where their bodies are never questioned. Jesus allows us to see life in the tombs, to see freedom, not in a shallow independence, but a holy interdependence—to see that our freedoms are intertwined. We will never have a true freedom if it requires the deportation, imprisonment, exile, or constant policing of another in order to make that freedom possible. We will never all be free until the flourishing of another's bodily life is the fruit of our mutual striving. Our bodies are more than an accumulation of cells, more than a mere cosmic accident. Our bodies are a song. They are words of love exchanged as new life is birthed and the lives of lost ones are carried on and on.

We cannot say we love God and justify the subjugation of some to death for misdemeanors, a society that spends more on security and national defense than it does to care for the birth, health, education, and old age of its citizens. The death of race is about the possibility of a true freedom in Christ—the freedom truly to live for one another, to honor one another's bodies as gifts, as holy reminders that God is mysterious and present, many and one. The body of Christ, the church, is not a spiritual space. The body of Christ is the union of our bodies—our histories, our unknowing, our gifts and fears and hopes oriented radically to the body of the Word that has come, and will come.

Our bodies and lives must be a new song. We are a body committed to confessing when we have failed to see either our beauty or our transgressions. And the tragic truth is that we need both in order to flourish. We are a body committed to this testimony in our eating, our tending, our learning, our voting, our working—in the advocacy of others, in the confession of how our lives, our families, our communities have resisted the lives of others.

And in the face of what feels like the constant dehumanization of this world, we speak words that create, build spaces where our whole selves can be known. We can sing these words in the streets and in church pews. We can stand in vestibules of power and declare, "If it does not make us all more human, more free, more loving, it is not worth doing."

But to do this we must come to see our words and our bodies together. We must see the geography of our towns and ask "Where are our tombs? Where are our swine?" We cannot be free until we confess our complicity in the binding of that poor man, until we recognize the ways that #AllLivesMatter is a lie in this world. To be free is to allow ourselves to be seen, to see that these ropes should not burn my ankles and that I was made for laughter and friendship and honest mistakes that are not punished with death, not desolate nights of mourning the women and men who should still be with us.

To live into the bodied love of Christ in a racial world, to build a new Christianity, we must imagine our bodies as words, as songs that sing an ancient song of God's promises. But this song is not about the repetition of rhythms and inflections that refashion the chains of our society's racialized thinking. No, this Christianity must live into the song of God's promise of presence that turns swords into plowshares, bends the blades that divide and fashions them into tools for the cultivation of life, making space in the earth for life and new birth. Our bodies and lives must be a new song.

This song is something like John Coltrane's 1961 version of "My Favorite Things." This iconic song of the Rodgers and Hammerstein musical "The Sound of Music" still reminds me of post-Christmas hot chocolate and the ideal of romping through the hills in familial bliss, leaving all of the nastiness of a Nazi regime far, far away. But in Coltrane's rendition only two years later, the hope remains within the horror. Coltrane's "My Favorite Things" takes place not upon the placid hills of a neutral borderland, but within the torment of a violent America, and his own conflicted soul.

Coltrane performs this song in a time when everything the black man or woman wants or desires is met with refusal and even hatred. They are thirsty, but there is a fountain they cannot drink from. To teach, to be a doctor, to travel, to hope for a home, a decent job, or simply believe that those who are meant to protect you will not kill you—these hopes are met with a declarative NO.

But in the midst of these refusals we find gaps. We find joy. We find one another. In this respect, to speak of my favorite things is to confess the joys, the small things that bring meaning to my life and comfort me in moments of fear or despair, but these things can never be spoken of in a tidy way. Underneath the laughter there's always a lingering knowledge of what the next day will bring.

Coltrane strips the melody down to its barest elements. Then, he fills in the gaps with inflections of pain and grief-tinged hope. In its subtracting and adding, "My Favorite Things" speaks the paradox of being black in America, in Coltrane's moment and in ours. Desires for peace, equality were always met with denials, hope with death, a cycle of finding enough in the scarcity and making something out of nothing. Like Coltrane's version of "My Favorite Things," the black experience in America is a story of taking something that was not meant for us, and making it speak of our humanity.

We create life out of what was meant to kill us. In the face of a white world our dark bodies that have always been a paradox continue to resist, surviving where we should die, finding joy where there should only be mourning, finding the courage to cry out in anger when our bodies are hated or cast aside. The cross is not a sign that suffering is redemptive. It is a sign that even the most deathly object can be bent into life. It is a sign that the crosses that torment us each day might be, could be, forged into life. This work is not an individual feat. The cross is the image of Jesus, his mother, and those who saw and believed, a communal confession, a public performance of God's artistic capacity to re-create, even from what is made for the cruelest of deaths.

Coltrane strips notes from one another, and then presses them together again in a different order. The stripping down and the reductions do not distort the song. His re-creating points to the paradox of our lives in America: having what we ought not to want, reaching toward what is not meant for us, trying to refuse the names and cages intended for us. Still, we sing that refrain of God's promise that never grows quiet.

In Coltrane's song we find new life, we find God. The misshapen song we believed about ourselves and our world is rearranged. Sometimes it is not us but our neighbor who is confronted with their own powerlessness and must cry out. Sometimes it is our neighbor who bears a quiet certainty that witnesses to God's faithfulness. Perhaps the question is not how do we order these two seemingly disparate moments, but rather what is it that prevents us from joining these disparate stories (and the people who so often exhibit them). The Christian life is not a question of ordering music or art, or thoughts, or step-by-step guides. The Christian life is becoming undone by a new social arrangement, being confronted with a new realization of the world around us, and those beside us.

It is this amalgamation of despair and possibility that I find so compelling within Coltrane's rendition. And while the song seemed rooted in a European ideal (or an American idealization of Europe), Coltrane's rendition speaks to what being human, what being Christian, could look like, mastering the form of a song's quiet longings but also wrapping that yearning within the deep pain of the present. Coltrane bent that song so that it could speak a new truth for us all.

Is it possible for Christians to reimagine themselves and their work alongside Coltrane's "My Favorite Things"? So many concerned for justice and mercy have found Christianity or at least its doctrine as the central culprit. But is it possible for us to utter this tune anew, to master the form so that we might deform the mastery?[1] Is it possible to think of liberation apart from the truth of God's enfleshment in the world as the truest deformation of enslavement we could know? This is the possibility of the Christian story. Perhaps theology (and our Christian lives) might be able to imagine the claims of the Christian faith anew, mastering its forms in order to unleash it for new work in a broken world whose privileged people have mistaken themselves for gods, as those who are sovereign, determining for themselves who they will be bound to.

Can our bodies and lives utter dissonant tones and the shrieking of righteous anger and yet still remind us of "our favorite things" even "when the dog bites, when the bee stings"?

I hope this is the case. We can sing this song and in a way that can remind creation of its calling in the midst of its unfaithfulness. Can we live in such a way that we reveal the freedom forged in Christ's life?

There is something powerful in the analogy of music. If race is a story, a song that demands that every note and every body cannot move, cannot be anything other than what the composer intended, perhaps we really are lost. Because how can we ever get to the truth of what a composer, someone long dead, meant or intended, could or could not see? But what if the composer wrote a song with enough structure to hold together and enough flexibility to be played in countless ways, again and again and again? What if our freedom was tied to being notes that found new resonances as they found new partners and new communities and new rhythms? What if race is just an ancient song that refuses to make sense of the

---

1. Professor of English and literary critic Houston Baker developed this idea to describe the poetry of the Harlem Renaissance.

beautiful depth and profundity of each dark dot that marks a score, a mystery that allows a body to slide and sound in new ways?

To be a Christian is to sing a new song. It is a song that speaks of our lives as images of God: bodies that do not know without the lives of others, bodies that reflect God in their need of a neighbor, bodies that eat and laugh and enjoy the world they are bound to. But there is no "new" without an "old." The old is the story that we cannot escape from. It is the story that lives along the streets that divide public housing from restored brownstones. It is the story of slavery and immigration, violence and violent silence. It is a story that feels alive today. And maybe to some it feels even truer than the resurrection.

The resurrection is the presence of our full humanity, our bodies reflecting the image of God. The death of race is not a hope for the overcoming of racial inequality alone. The death of race is the beginning of recognizing the fullness of our bodied lives and how we cannot neatly separate the various particularities of our bodies from one another. What gave rise to racism is what lives in sexism, patriarchy, homophobia, and ableism. It persists in rhetoric of sexuality that resists the possibilities of covenantal love in same-sex relationships. It lurks underneath Christian rhetoric of nationalism and the so-called illegal alien.

If the church must decide between being racially diverse and allowing women to preach, if it seeks racial justice but cannot reimagine the place of queer bodies among us, we become a church without a body, an idea that floats above the comingling of dirt and Spirit, blind to the mysterious differences and likenesses of our holy bodies. We cannot choose what aspects of the body are palatable to us. Jesus's body overturns every notion of propriety to be with us. If we are to participate in God's overcoming the death of race, we will need more than a multicultural congregation. We will need the transfigured body of Christ. We will need a body that eats fish with friends one moment and walks with us, hidden, in another. We need a body that is familiar and a body that is strange. We need a body that confesses its beauty, its transgression, its guilt, or its worth—in its daily life as it discovers new ways of being for one another, of being with one another. As we do, we might begin to see new ways of refusing that de-creating word, race, and utter old words with new meaning.

If our lives are going to confess that rebirth, newness, is truly possible, we must live as if the resurrection is true. But this will require us to sing, to utter with our bodies a strange and beautiful sound. This is a sound that cannot come from the *idea* of a song. We must breathe in, let the air fill our lungs and tuck our belly in, then let the sound out, let it rattle our throats and pour into the world not knowing if it is in tune. To sing a new song requires your body, your mind, and your soul. To sing a new song requires you to acknowledge that there is something you don't know, but need to know. To sing a new song is to accustom your ears to sounds and ways of moving your mouth that seem unnatural. But most of all, to sing a new song requires a radical commitment to making sure that all are free to sing along with you. The choir needs difference, it needs all the parts; the story needs all the tellers to be truthful, to be whole. To be a Christ follower in this moment is to fight the death of race so that the life of God might be felt for all.

Epilogue

I have been struggling to find the words to end this book. Each day seems to bring a new, traumatizing reminder of just how deeply race has afflicted our society and our world. As I was searching I came across a letter I had written to my son when he was twelve. He had just begun to hear the history of race in America and had begun to feel its complicated violence in his tiny middle school world. As I read these words again I could not help but think they were the only words I have left, that perhaps they were not only for my children, but also for me, and maybe you.

To my beloved son,

You were only ten years old when you saw that American miracle: Barack Obama sworn into office as president of the United States of America. Innocence seemed to be reclaimed in that moment as so many heard, in the president's oath, centuries of guilt absolved. "To a post-racial future!" some exclaimed, hopeful for a unity that seemed so difficult to grasp even in our so-called enlightened time.

And yet, two years later you have come to discover the true "curse of Ham," the refusal of difference that ferments beneath the surface of every society, that reveals us all to be more savage than civil. You have now glimpsed just how much we humans thrive on difference, how we seek it out even in its most subtle forms (and that seventh-graders seem particularly adept at!).

But, as these realities seem to so often reveal, our present is never quite the simple repetition of the past. You, the child of a mulatto man and a Korean American mother, are the sum of many parts, places, stories, and possibilities. In so many ways you encapsulate what many people hope for when they imagine a "post-racial" future.

It has pained me so to see you discover that post-racial is, in sad fact, simply a poor recalibration of an awkward arrangement made long, long ago when there were only whites and coloreds. You have stumbled into a world where a few white boys will exclude you, call you black because you are not white, and where a Latino boy can call you a nigger without the slightest hesitation, his ignorance or his malice equally troubling crimes.

So here you are, in post-racial America.

This does not have to be the end of the story, the end of our possibilities. But you should know the world you have entered and what peculiar space you occupy. Welcome to the nebulous space of the inter, the in-between, the not quite—to racial ambiguity.

In the first twelve years of your life, the question of who or what you were was a pleasantry, a curiosity. But now you are beginning to feel how innocent questions of your identity seem to have more attached to them than you realized. Not looking Asian enough to be easily absorbed into the Asian table, not dark enough to find a place with the black kids, and, as some have felt willingly enough to tell you to your face, too dark to be white. Welcome son, to the neither/nor.

You are not the first and not the last to feel the constriction of this space. In fact, you are now a second-generation "in-betweener," and sadly the world some of us hoped would emerge, where the curiosity of the mulatto, the half-breed would be no more, is still not here.

If left to ourselves perhaps we could hope for the space to become true individuals, to become our full selves apart from what others desire us to be or without the chains of cultural expectation.

But our world is not a world of endless possibilities and autonomous individuals. You and I are bound to each other. You and I are tied to those who refuse us and those who welcome us. All of these histories, realities, wellsprings of cultural achievement and tragedy flow through your veins, in your face.

You and I are people of the in-between, people who cannot easily seek to be simply "who we are" because our "who" is inexplicable without these peoples. Our life is not our own. We belong to many peoples but above all we belong to God (of course you knew this was coming!). This makes us what some Christians have called "foreigners in every fatherland, and in every foreign land, a citizen."

If being post-racial means anything, perhaps it is this: that we are always at home, and we are never home. If being a Christian means anything, it is that we are always at home, and we are never home and because of this, the exclusion, the refusals we so often endure, are never the entirety of our lives.

Much love,

Your father

I do not have lists of best practices or policies. I do not have a step-by-step guide on how to overcome individual or systemic racism. But in the face of these overwhelming realities, also know that people change and that social systems are not immune to God's justice. Everything can, and will change. But will this change open up possibilities for those whose lives are marginalized? Will this change create a world where we can see ourselves more truthfully and live among one another with a freedom that participates in God's life? I believe so. I believe so because I have seen people fill streets and risk their life to interrupt our distorted social systems. I believe so because I see the strength of people and communities who, day after day, survive despite a society bent on their destruction. I believe because I see a growing body of people, from all stories and races and ethnicities, beginning to demand dignity and inclusion in a society built upon the supremacy of the white body.

But above all, I believe so because at the center of my faith is a God whose body has broken into our condition and shown me that love is a life of stretching my body toward another, pressing for their wholeness even as they fight for mine. God's body has brought death to race; now we must embody life. This is the Christian story.

Suggested Reading

This book was just a beginning. To see ourselves and God more truthfully, we must also be willing to discover our story alongside other people's stories. We must learn to speak truthfully with others. To do this we must also begin to discover the resources and the beauty of different stories, and see their histories in ours. The following is a list of ways to continue the journey, including histories, literature, theories of race, reflections on Jesus, and readings of Christian Scripture from diverse perspectives.

Race is a story

Part of reimagining our Christian identity in a racial world begins with understanding how race and identity more broadly actually *work*. The following books are examinations help us to see race as a complicated process and how the history of race develops over time, shaping our world and who we are.

Jennings, Willie James. *The Christian Imagination: Theology and the Origins of Race*. New Haven: Yale University Press, 2010.

Jordan, Winthrop D. *The White Man's Burden: Historical Origins of Racism in the United States*. New York: Oxford University Press, 1974.

Markus, Hazel Rose, and Paula M. L. Moya. *Doing Race: 21 Essays for the 21st Century*. 1st ed. New York/London: W. W. Norton, 2010.

Morrison, Toni. *Playing in the Dark: Whiteness and the Literary Imagination*. William E. Massey Sr. Lectures in the History of American Civilization. Cambridge, MA: Harvard University Press, 1992.

Who is Jesus?

Jesus is the central figure of what it means to be a Christian. But if we are to imagine what Christianity could look like in a racial world we need to draw from the insight of those whose bodies and lives are so profoundly shaped by race in direct ways. These books are excellent starting points to see Christ through various lenses, to imagine his person and work in new ways.

Bantum, Brian. *Redeeming Mulatto: A Theology of Race and Christian Hybridity*. Waco, TX: Baylor University Press, 2010.

Copeland, M. Shawn. *Enfleshing Freedom: Body, Race, and Being*. Innovations. Minneapolis: Fortress Press, 2010.

Thurman, Howard. *Jesus and the Disinherited*. New York: Abingdon-Cokesbury, 1949.

Twiss, Richard. *Rescuing the Gospel from the Cowboys: A*

Native American Expression of the Jesus Way. Downers Grove, IL: InterVarsity, 2015.

Douglas, Kelly Brown. *Stand Your Ground: Black Bodies and the Justice of God*. Maryknoll, NY: Orbis 2015.

Rereading our story

The story of the Christian life and the Bible shapes how we think we ought to live. Looking at these stories, whether in Scripture or the history of the church, we begin to see new opportunities to embody the freedom of God's kingdom in the world.

Gutiérrez, Gustavo. *On Job: God-talk and the Suffering of the Innocent*. Maryknoll, NY: Orbis, 1987.

Higginbotham, Evelyn Brooks. *Righteous Discontent: The Women's Movement in the Black Baptist Church, 1880-1920*. 1st paperback ed. Cambridge, MA: Harvard University Press, 1994.

Isasi-Díaz, Ada María. *Mujerista Theology: A Theology for the Twenty-first Century*. Maryknoll, NY: Orbis, 1996.

Kim, Grace Ji-Sun. *Embracing the Other: The Transformative Spirit of Love*. Prophetic Christianity. Grand Rapids: Eerdmans, 2015.

Raboteau, Albert J. *Canaan Land: A Religious History of African Americans*. New York: Oxford University Press, 2001.

Rah, Soong-Chan. *The Next Evangelicalism: Releasing the Church from Western Cultural Captivity*. Downers Grove, IL: InterVarsity, 2009.

Smith, Mitzi J. *I Found God in Me: A Womanist Biblical Hermeneutics Reader*. Eugene, OR: Cascade, 2015.

Toyama-Szeto, Nikki A., and Tracey Gee. *More Than Serving Tea: Asian American Women on Expectations, Relationships, Leadership and Faith*. Downers Grove, IL: InterVarsity, 2006.

Williams, Delores S. *Sisters in the Wilderness: The Challenge of Womanist God-talk*. Maryknoll, NY: Orbis, 2013.

Literature

While many people consider theology to have God as its explicit center, in order to understand God *and God's world*, we must also hear the voices of people who are careful and skilled observers of the human condition. Their words and insights can cut and inspire, helping us to see ourselves and our world in new ways.

Baldwin, James. *The Fire Next Time*. New York: Dial, 1963.

Kingston, Maxine Hong. *The Woman Warrior: Memoirs of a Girlhood among Ghosts*. New York: Vintage, 1977.

Morrison, Toni. *The Bluest Eye*. New York: Plume, 1994.

Ng, Celeste. *Everything I Never Told You*. New York: Penguin, 2014.

Rankine, Claudia. *Citizen: An American Lyric*. Minneapolis: Graywolf, 2014.

Rodriguez, Richard. *Brown: The Last Discovery of America*. New York: Penguin, 2003.

Smith, Zadie. *Changing My Mind: Occasional Essays*. New York: Penguin, 2009.